San Rafael

In the first centuries after the birth of Christ, a unique civilization rose out of Central America's tropical forests. The Mayan people created an agricultural society and built spectacular religious centers that served as hubs of vast, densely populated regions. They managed these feats in a jungle environment totally unsuited to the growth of cities and the successful practice of farming, and did so with only the most basic technology at their disposal.

Centuries later, some of the Mayan centers became the sites of Spanish–American colonial cities. *San Rafael*, an invented metropolis built on the site of the fictitious Mayan center *Uaxacmal*, on the banks of the equally fictitious *Xunantun River*, is a close approximation of one of those cities. Its site could be anywhere in the region that lies south of Mexico's Yucatán Peninsula and north of Guatemala's Sierra de las Minas, an area that includes the Mexican state of Chiapas, Guatemala's central region, southern Belize, and western Honduras.

Uaxacmal rose over the course of several centuries and slowly developed as the political, administrative, and religious center of a huge region settled by the Mayas. Architecture, painting, sculpture, astronomy, mathematics, and writing flourished in the dense tropical forests, until, in the space of only a few years, the Mayan civilization collapsed and Uaxacmal was devoured by the jungle.

After the collapse, a new chapter began, and the urban adventure continued. Spanish conquistadors arrived and laid the foundation for a colonial city: San Rafael. A new way of life spread throughout the Americas, a product of the encounter — or rather the collision — between Europe and the New World. San Rafael was both protagonist and witness to this process.

Copyright © 1992 by Editoriale Jaca Book SpA
First American edition 1992
Originally published in Italy in 1992 by Editoriale Jaca Book SpA
English translation by Kathleen Leverich copyright © 1992 by Houghton Mifflin Company

Printed in Italy

10 9 8 7 6 5 4 3 2 1

Library of Congress Cataloging-in-Publication Data

Hernández, Xavier, 1954-
    San Rafael : a Central American city through the ages / Xavier
Hernandez ; illustrated by Jordi Ballonga and Josep Escofet ;
translated by Kathleen Leverich. — 1st American ed.
      p. cm.
    "Originally published in Italy in 1992 by Editorial Jaca Book SpA" —
T.p. verso.
    Summary: Describes the development of a fictional city in Central
America from 1000 B.C. to the late twentieth century.
    ISBN 0-395-60645-4
    1. Cities and towns—Central America—History—Juvenile literature.
[1. Cities and towns—Central America—History.] I. Ballonga, Jordi,
ill. II. Escofet, Josep, ill. III. Title.
HT128.A2H47 1992
307.76'09728—dc20   91-39906
                                                 CIP
                                                   AC

SAN RAFAEL

A Central American City Through the Ages

Xavier Hernández

Illustrated by
Jordi Ballonga and Josep Escofet

Translated by Kathleen Leverich

Houghton Mifflin Company
Boston 1992

1. Jaguar's Roar: 1000 B.C.

1. Jaguar's Roar
1000 B.C.

One thousand years before the birth of Christ, native peoples descended from the Sierra Madre in what is now the Mexican state of Chiapas, and from Guatemala's high plains, and migrated to the jungle lowlands to the north. These people carried with them a precious treasure: corn, the highly nutritious cereal plant that formed the basis of their diet. Corn was unknown outside of the Americas, where the indigenous peoples had developed it from wild grains through a long and complex process of hybridization.

One of the migrant groups settled beside the large Xunantun River, in a region where the mountains' last soft foothills melted harmoniously into the tropical forest. There the mountain people set about clearing jungle land for the cultivation of corn.

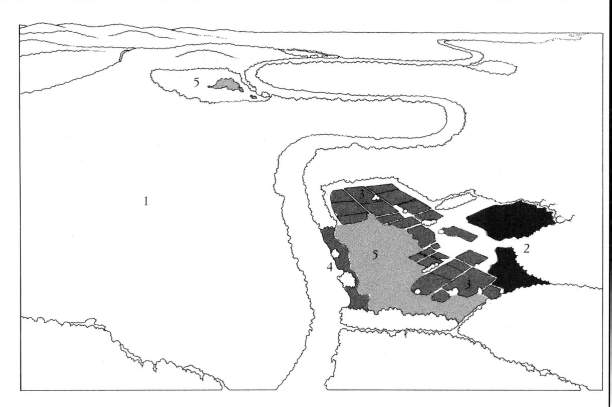

1. Jungle
The jungle is a region of dense vegetation. The foliage of its soaring trees forms a canopy through which sunlight filters only faintly. On the jungle floor, shrubs and ground covers compete for the scarce light. The lowlands are a maze of marshes, bogs, streams, and stagnant ponds.

2. Deforested zones
Settlers cleared forest land for cultivation by burning off the vegetation. The region's humid climate made this difficult work. Tracts often required repeated burnings to rid them of all growth. Stump removal was also a major undertaking. The settlers dug around the roots, tied ropes to the stump, and pulled it up.

3. Milpas
Corn was and is the staple food of Central America. Corn fields, and by extension all fields under cultivation, were called milpas. *When the soil of a* milpa *was exhausted by successive harvests, the land was abandoned for new fields. In many cases it would have been more practical to enrich the established* milpa *with mud from the river.*

4. Jetty
Because travel through the jungle was difficult, rivers became the easiest and most rapid avenues of communication. Dugout canoes or canoes made of rush were the vessels best adapted to jungle travel.

5. Village
Villages offered protection from the jungle's dangers. Huts and granaries made of plant matter and mud were structures typical of this first stage of urban development.

Agriculture
Settlers used *coas*, or planting sticks, to sow the fields. Central American farmers were skilled from the earliest times at developing new crops by improving plants found in the wild. The most important of these was hybrid corn; others included chilis, squashes, beans, several varieties of tubers, cacao, vanilla, breadfruit, and *zapotes* or sapodilla plums.

The project was filled with difficulties. The vegetation was dense, and insects and vermin were numerous. The roar of the jaguars that patroled the jungle made the settlers wary. They revered the great cats as gods and passed on this reverence to succeeding generations.

In a small clearing near the river, the settlers established temporary encampments and later built the first huts, of logs and vegetation. All huts were the same. In this egalitarian society, leaders had the same obligations and privileges as other members of the group. Once boats were built, the river provided an easy avenue of communication with other settlements.

Enormous efforts were required to clear small parcels of jungle so that planting could begin. The farmers burned the vegetation, cleared the debris, and pulled up any tree stumps that remained. Their only tools were poles, wooden and obsidian adzes and hoes, and rope made from agave fibers, or pita. They used *coas*, or digging poles, to till the soil for the first corn crop. While they awaited the harvest, the settlers relied on the jungle to furnish the fruits and game they needed to survive.

With the passage of years, corn crops increased. More and more forest tracts were cleared and planted; the settlers selected high ground that offered good drainage. They used river mud to fertilize the fields. Slowly the farmers added other crops: cacao, beans, breadfruit, and squashes. They won the first battle with the jungle. Through backbreaking labor, they transformed the hostile environment into the setting for a new civilization.

Deforestation
Clearing jungle was a laborious task. First the vegetation was burned off. Some trees would burn only after being kindled with dry wood. The farmers then pulled up the remaining stumps with ropes and obsidian adzes. These adzes were also useful in clearing the burned tract of debris. The ashes of the burned vegetation were spread over the soil as fertilizer.

2. Temples in the Jungle: 3rd Century B.C.

2. Temples in the Jungle
3rd Century B.C.

With the passage of time, larger areas of jungle were cleared and cultivated. As the settlement's population grew, however, a shortage of fertile tracts developed, and ownership disputes became common. With increasing frequency, priests intervened to settle matters of land distribution.

The development of agriculture and the development of religious practices were in fact directly linked. Farmers prayed to various gods of the natural world for good harvests. Some individuals devoted themselves increasingly to religious rituals, and as priests claimed the role of intermediaries between their neighbors and the gods. The priests studied the stars to establish a calendar; this enabled them to predict the best times of the year for planting and harvesting crops. Their astronom-

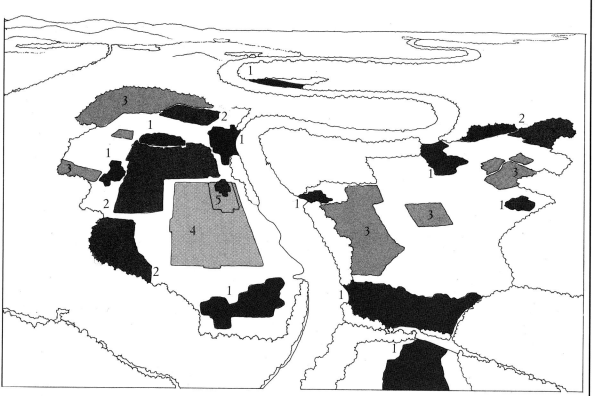

1. Villages
The population grew slowly but continuously. As fields were exhausted and their yield fell below what was needed to feed a village's population, new settlements were built nearby.

2. New cultivated areas
The depletion of the milpas through successive harvests forced villagers to clear new, more distant fields. At the same time, the needs of a growing population meant that the size of the areas under cultivation had to be increased. Corn, legumes, and other vegetables were the most common crops.

3. Abandoned land
Repeated cultivation depleted the fields of vital nutrients. Some fields could be fertilized with the river's rich mud, but when this failed to regenerate them, they had to be abandoned, at least temporarily, to renew themselves. After a few years they were burned and cleared again, and returned to cultivation.

4. Platform
The construction of temples and related buildings required, as a first step, the creation of a broad, solid platform. The land was leveled and packed. A platform big enough to provide space for the future construction of additional temples served as a site for large ritual gatherings that lent cohesion to the community.

5. Small pyramid and temple
The first Mayan temples stood on the summits of small step pyramids. There the priests could celebrate the various rites within view of enormous gatherings of worshipers.

Manufactured goods
The Mayas were unacquainted with the wheel and so did not have the benefit of the potter's wheel in fashioning ceramics. They baked pottery in kilns or bonfires. Although the Mayas lacked knowledge of metallurgy, they were able to make tools of obsidian or flint. They wove cloth on belt looms.

ical observations and their calendars were remarkably precise, and their agricultural predictions proved correct for many years.

The priests acquired enormous power and prestige with their authority to redistribute land and harvests. They gradually became the leaders of the settlement and the deciding voices in all matters of production, distribution, and trade. Each farmer reported the harvest from his *milpa* and was required to turn over to the priests all but what his family needed to survive. The priests redistributed or traded the surplus.

Because farm work was seasonal, farmers had four or five months each year to devote to other tasks. The priests organized public works teams to build the first temples, honoring the various gods. Hundreds of farmers from surrounding villages leveled the land of a well-drained area near the river. They transported huge quantities of stone to build a large platform and a small stepped pyramid, which they topped with a temple roofed with palm leaves. The pyramid, which was visible from many points along the river and within the jungle, strengthened the sense of community among people in the surrounding villages. It served also as a reminder of the powerful gods who protected the community.

This religious center, called Uaxacmal, was one of several in the region. In other parts of the jungle, in other communities, the same phenomenon was occurring. The gray-and-white stone structures of the religious centers soon dotted the green jungle. These were the forerunners of the Mayan civilization.

Mayan huts

The Mayas created a type of hut that was replicated unchanged for centuries. They built the hut on a stone platform that protected it from the soil's moisture. It was basically rectangular in shape, although the two shorter sides were convex rather than flat. The frame was built of logs; the walls, of a combination of cane, branches, and mud. The roof was made of vegetable fibers. The family's few household goods included a hearth, looms for weaving cotton fabric, hand grinders, and straw sleeping mats.

① Walls of branches, cane, and mud
② Roof of palm leaves
③ Stone platform
④ Hand mill for grinding cacao, corn, and other grains
⑤ Loom
⑥ Hearth for the preparation of corn tortillas and other foods

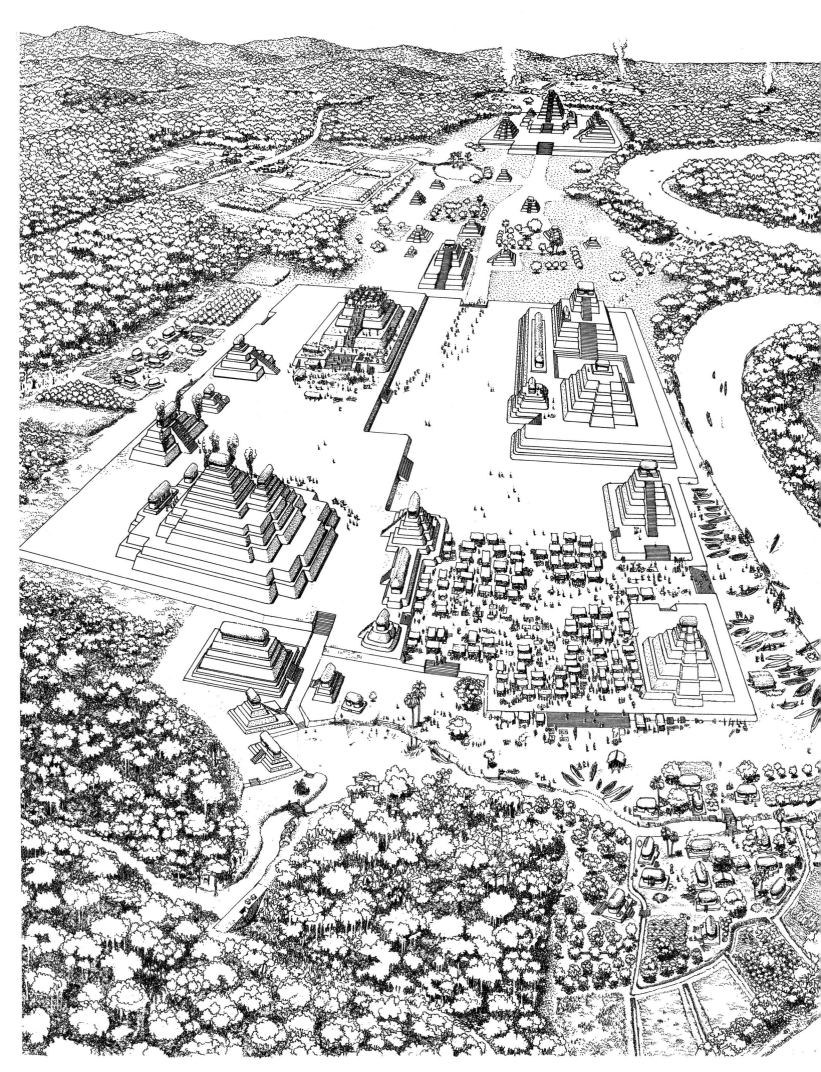

3. Pyramids to the Sky: 4th Century A.D.

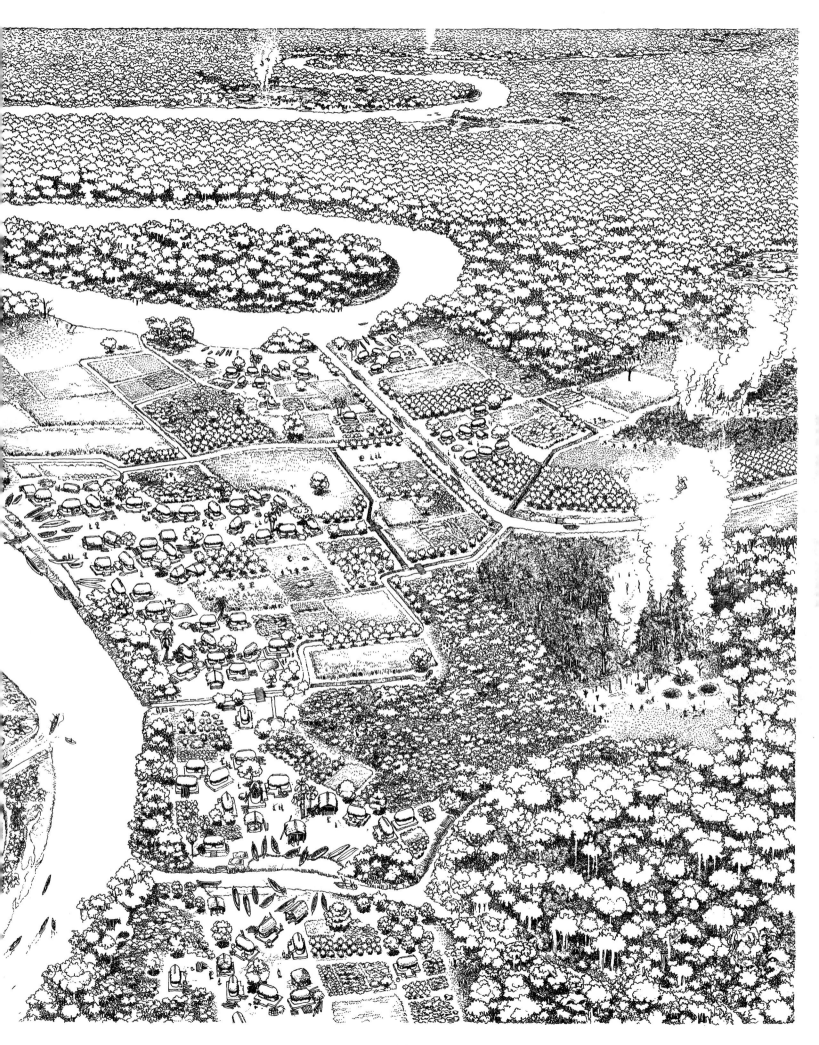

3. Pyramids to the Sky

4th Century A.D.

Uaxacmal gradually became the most important Mayan religious center of the region. Its priests ruled the many villages scattered along the banks and in the valley of the Xunantun. As the capital of a small Mayan state, it became an active participant in the cultural development of the region south of the Yucatán.

On religious holidays, hundreds of people from distant villages traveled to Uaxacmal to participate in rites honoring the gods. In addition to their religious significance, these gatherings offered an opportunity for the people of far-flung villages to meet and trade.

The priests established themselves as the supreme civil and religious authorities of a society scattered throughout the tropical forest. They requisitioned crops to finance the work of artisans, who produced sump-

1. Temple pyramids
The key symbol of the Mayan religious center was its pyramids. They rose ever taller and each was surmounted by a small sanctuary. Because they were visible from great distances, they served as a point of reference throughout the jungle, and also reminded all who saw them of the gods' constant presence.

2. Plazas
The religious centers included plazas that were broad enough to hold the huge crowds that gathered on ceremonial days. From the plaza the people could follow the sacred rites that the priests performed at the top of the pyramid.

3. Water supplies
Large cisterns or tanks assured the religious centers of ample water supplies, both in quiet times and during feast days.

4. Cacao plantations
Some Mayan states established plantations devoted to the cultivation of cacao and other products. Priests set aside part of the harvests for sacred rites, part for export, and part for their own use.

5. Canals
The construction of a network of canals provided a major boost to the culture and economy. The canals permitted rapid communication by boat. Materials required for enlarging the religious centers could be transported by water. The canal systems also permitted efficient irrigation of cultivated areas.

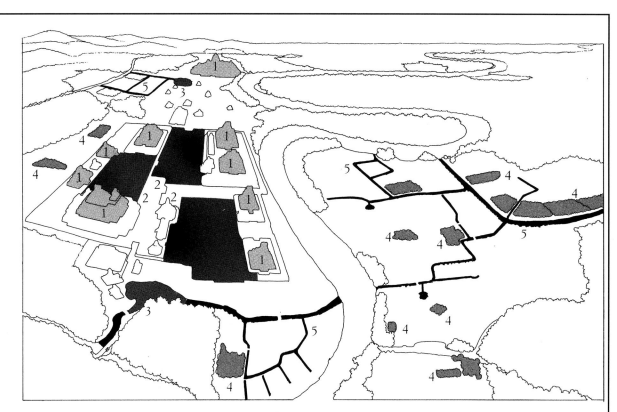

Construction materials
The Mayas were gifted builders and masons. Their building material of choice was stone. Stonemasons squared blocks with hammers fashioned from stone. Occasionally, builders used adobe bricks. Mortar was prepared by crushing limestone and mixing the powder with water and sand. The mortar was used to cement stones together and to plaster the outer building surfaces.

tuous goods for the priests, their families, and the Mayan state's commercial trade. In addition, the state established cotton, cacao, and fig plantations and offered the harvests in trade.

Stable trade relations began to develop with more distant Mayan centers and with other Central American peoples. From the high plateau of Chiapas and Guatemala, Uaxacmal imported jade, obsidian, hematite, cinnabar, diorite, brilliantly colored feathers from the quetzal (a tropical bird), and hand mills fashioned of volcanic rock. Salt and purple dye arrived from the Pacific coast. In exchange, Uaxacmal exported pottery, flint tools, jade objects, furs, cotton, feathers, cocoa, wax, and honey.

The governing group organized a variety of public works. They set up state-run plantations and built large canals in the forest, both to ease

transport and to provide irrigation for the *milpas*. They commandeered their people's manual labor to expand the religious center. The platforms were extended, and new, taller pyramids were built on them. The ancient pyramids provided bases for grander structures. In the midst of the jungle, Uaxacmal was becoming an extensive and imposing temple complex.

Still, Uaxacmal was not a city. For the most part, its buildings and avenues were deserted or semideserted, since only the priests and their assistants lived in the religious center. Only on feast days, when the population of the region crowded the esplanades to watch the sacred rites and hear the directives of the priests, did Uaxacmal come to life.

Pyramid construction
The first step in building a pyramid was to level and pack the earth. Then the tiers were raised, under the direction of an architect. During seasonal lulls in agricultural work, large numbers of farmers supplied labor for the construction. They transported baskets filled with stones of every shape and size, often from remote locations. Large scaffolds aided in the work. The pyramid was plastered and painted in vivid colors. Plaster was also used as a finishing agent on the bas-reliefs that adorned several sections of the pyramid.

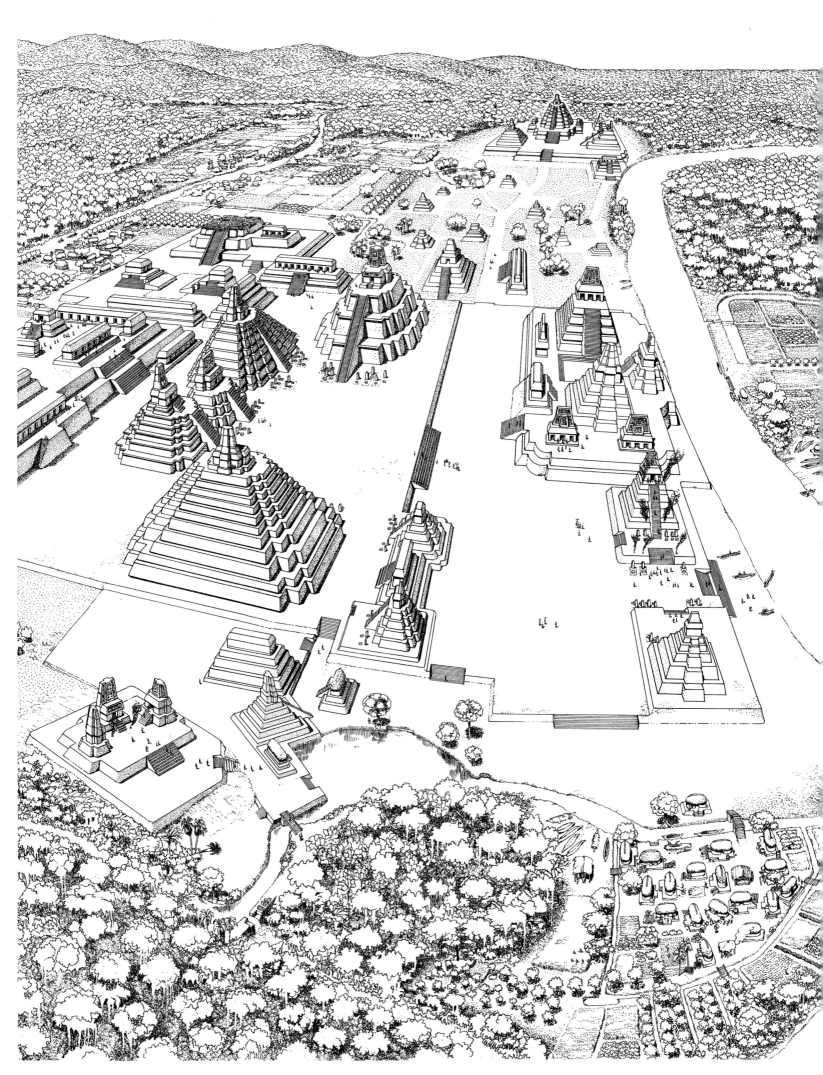

4. Empire on the River: 7th Century

4. Empire on the River
7th Century

In the mid-seventh century, Uaxacmal entered the period of its greatest achievements and influence. One powerful leader held the position of *halach uinic*, or absolute ruler, of the entire Uaxacmal district. The heirs of the ruling dynasties succeeded one another in that position, often erecting steles, or stone monuments, in their own honor. Under the late seventh-century leadership of the *halach uinic* Jaguar-Iguana and Armor of the Sun, the religious center became a place of permanent residence for a growing population.

In all the lands held by the Mayas, a unique civilization coalesced. There were major achievements in the sciences, largely because this society of farmers needed precise knowledge of agricultural cycles. Exhaustive studies of the celestial bodies were carried out, and systems

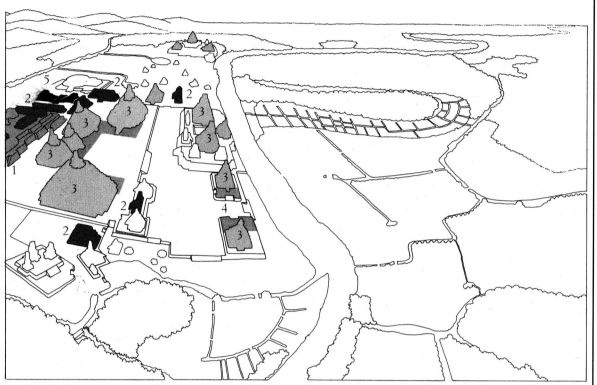

1. Citadel
A series of graduated stone terraces occupied by outbuildings and dwellings gave the religious center the appearance of a citadel. Buildings appeared to be multistory but were not. Each one stood independently on the graduated terraces.

2. Palaces
The nobles, governors, priests, and their dependents resided in specific parts of the religious center. Splendid palaces were built in the most elevated areas.

3. Pyramids
New step-pyramids, with a single access stairway, proliferated in the ceremonial centers. Some were created as funerary monuments to outstanding leaders. The tomb rested in an interior chamber reached by narrow corridors. The pyramids were surmounted by small temples that had elaborate stone bas-reliefs on their summits.

4. Steles
Steles, or stone monuments sculpted in honor of particular rulers, were erected throughout the religious center, particularly at the bases of pyramids. The steles were inscribed with information about the most important events of the period.

5. Pelota
The game of pelota *spread throughout Central America, and the Mayas were among its most* enthusiastic players and spectators. Teams faced each other in an enclosed court and hurled a rubber ball back and forth.

Carving of steles
The commemorative steles honoring illustrious rulers were large monoliths, often transported from distant locations, that artisans incised in bas-relief with stone chisels. Their hieroglyphic inscriptions detailed the most important events of the period.

of writing and arithmetic were developed in order to create a useful, accurate calendar. The Mayan arithmetic system was based on the number 20 and included the sophisticated concept of zero. Calculations of every type were possible. Knowledge and use of hieroglyphic writing was restricted to the Mayan priests. Texts were set down in bas-relief on stone or in codices on paper made from the leaves and fibers of the agave plant. The Mayas' scientific and technical advances were notable. They discovered how to use rubber as well as the natural dyes in logwood, the indigo plant, the purple mollusk, and the cochineal insect. They built magnificent boulevards. Their waterworks were also noteworthy.

Art flourished during this period, especially mural painting, painted ceramics, sculpture, and stone bas-relief work. Mayan architecture also arrived at its zenith. The Mayas succeeded in creating stone roofs for their buildings by constructing reinforced vaults based on approximations worked out in thread. A new series of buildings transformed Uaxacmal. Ancient pyramids were enlarged, and new ones were erected. On the summits stood temples adorned with bold stone battlements. Palaces were built in the religious compound for the use of the rulers and their immediate dependents. In the city center, the construction of graduated terraces created an imposing citadel.

For the people's entertainment, *pelota* courts were built. The crowds that assembled on feast days passionately followed the matches. Lively markets were held with increasing frequency. The most important achievement of the period, however, may have been the enlargement of the ambitious network of irrigation and transport canals.

Uaxacmal stood at the center of a small river empire that had created an advanced agrarian civilization in the hostile jungle.

Pyramids as mausoleums
In many cases the bodies of illustrious rulers were entombed in pyramids. The body was placed, along with precious funerary offerings, in a chamber in the heart of the structure. Access to the chamber was gained through narrow tunnels that were afterward blocked with great stone slabs.

Funerary chambers
The members of the ruling classes were buried with elaborate ceremony in carefully prepared subterranean chambers. The chamber walls were decorated with frescoes. Ceramics, jewels, jade carvings, and other precious objects were entombed beside the body.

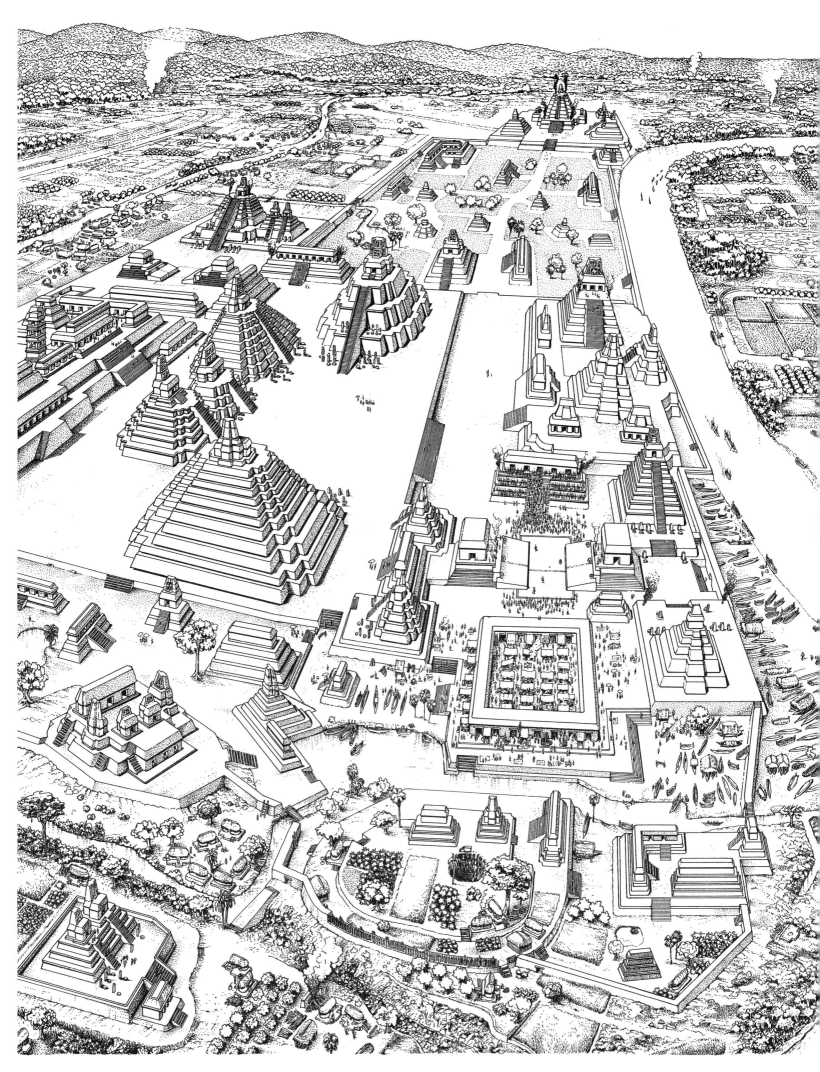

5. Splendor of a Mayan City: Late 9th Century

5. Splendor of a Mayan City
Late 9th Century

During the seventh and eighth centuries, Uaxacmal continued its slow growth. From one generation to the next, the city barely changed. Villages multiplied in the jungle, however, and the religious center grew steadily more elaborate and magnificent.

The population continued to build and enlarge pyramids and palaces in the by now ancient tradition. New *pelota* courts were built, and small private residences for the nobility were constructed on the city outskirts. Each of these dwellings was provided with its own small temple.

In contrast to the custom in earlier periods, many people closely connected to the priests and nobility lived permanently in Uaxacmal. These included stonecutters; weavers; craftspeople who worked with jewels, furs, or feathers; toolmakers; architects; and traders. A plaza enclosed by

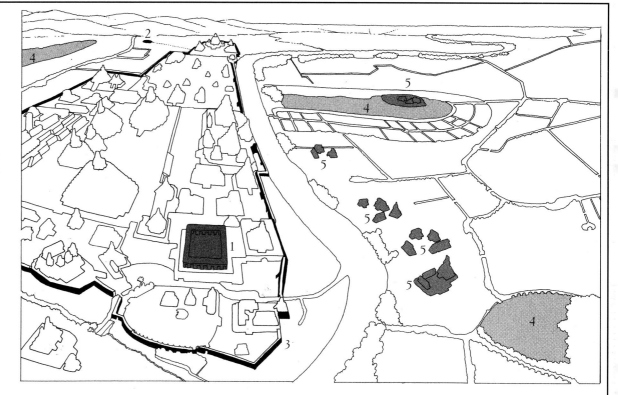

1. Marketplace
Buildings with multiple entryways surrounded the rectangular plaza that served as a more or less permanent market. In periods when the city received major influxes of people from the surrounding country, smaller markets sprang up in other locations.

2. Cenote
The cenote, *or sacred well, was the site of important rituals. The priests cast jewels and other precious objects into it as sacrifices to the gods. Men and women were also drowned there in sacrifice.*

3. Defensive walls
Struggles between the several Mayan states as well as incursions of other hostile peoples caused many Mayan centers to build defensive walls.

4. Terraced fields
By grading successive levels of nearby hillsides to form tiers, or terraces, the Mayas created new fields to feed the rapidly growing population.

5. Residences of the nobility
Powerful nobles frequently built homes and private granaries on the outskirts of the religious center. They may have organized peasants to work their land in the same way that powerful colonial landholders would do centuries later.

Marketplace
The Mayas did not have a monetary system, although some highly prized commodities—cacao, jade, copal—served as a basis of exchange. Nearly all commerce was based on the barter system. Many manufactured products were available in the lively markets.

four rectangular buildings served as the city marketplace.

During religious festivals, Uaxacmal took on the appearance of a densely populated metropolis. The city was jammed with people who had come to participate in the religious rites and sacrifices, to watch *pelota* matches, or to wander through the markets. As in the past, the priests handed down their directives from the heights of the pyramids, and offered human sacrifices to the gods in the *cenote*, or sacred well.

In spite of its apparent prosperity during the ninth century, Uaxacmal began to show the first signs of a society in crisis. The population grew at an alarming rate, making it necessary for farmers to clear more jungle land and constantly increase the production of land already under cultivation. They were eventually forced to create terraced fields on nearby mountainsides. In spite of these efforts, food production barely sufficed to feed the population, and in years of poor harvests people suffered terrible famines.

The shadow of war also fell over the region. Warriors from neighboring states repeatedly attacked Uaxacmal's territory to steal its food stores. In addition, warlike peoples from distant regions periodically invaded the jungle, bringing devastation with them. To defend themselves against these threats, Uaxacmal's people built an enclosing wall around the religious center. The city's warrior class grew in prestige and importance and eventually challenged the old nobility's authority. The priests, who had always wielded enormous political power, lost influence and clashed in their turn with the new warrior aristocracy. The peasant population was obliged to feed ever more numerous upper-class groups with diminishing harvest surpluses. These circumstances led to Uaxacmal's demise.

Pelota
The game of *pelota* has fascinated Central America's diverse peoples for centuries. The Mayas were passionate fans. Two teams competed in a specially built court. Players had to strike the rubber ball using only their hips and forearms. Spectators watching from steps or terraces surrounding the court rooted for their favorites, and perhaps gambled on the results of the match.

6. Jungle Swallows Stone: 14th Century

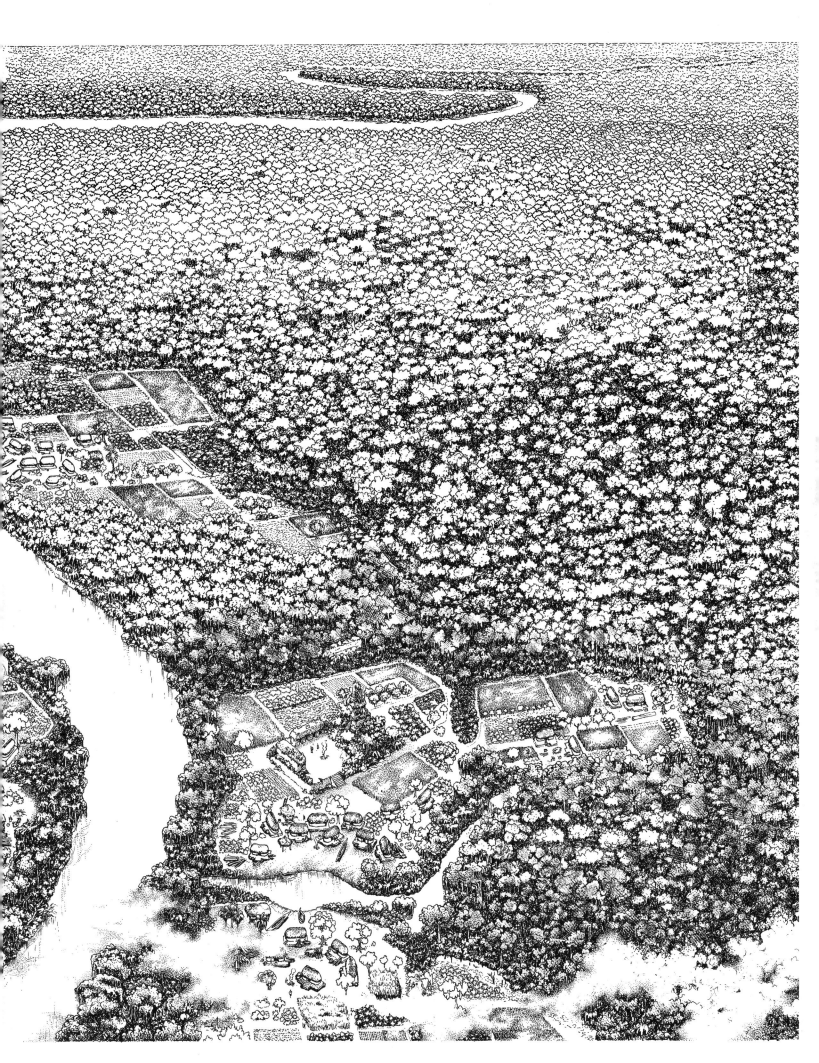

6. Jungle Swallows Stone
14th Century

By the end of the fourteenth century, Uaxacmal was a dead city; only a few overgrown mounds and some barely visible stone ruins recalled its former glory. The religious center, canals, and fields had all been reclaimed by the jungle.

Uaxacmal was unable to overcome the grave crises that afflicted it from the close of the ninth century: population growth; depletion of fields; internal struggles among the nobility; invasions by other peoples. In only a few years the small jungle empire had fallen into ruin. Hunger became a way of life for the farmers. Rulers resorted to violence to obtain their accustomed tribute. The result was a profound social crisis. Continuing wars disrupted the flow of trade, and little by little, the entire Xunantun Valley slipped into isolation. Powerful trade centers

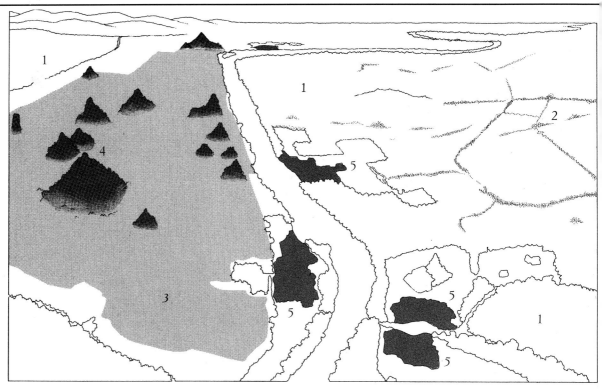

1. Overgrown fields
When cultivated fields were abandoned, surrounding vegetation quickly encroached. The underbrush took over first, followed by shrubs and trees. Soon the fields were completely reintegrated into the forest.

2. Canal ruins
Once the canals ceased to be tended, silt began to accumulate. The channels were reduced to stagnant pools overgrown with vegetation. With time, soil filled in, and a gentle dip in the earth remained as the only evidence of the great engineering project realized by the Mayas.

3. Buried palaces and streets
The jungle took some years to overwhelm the city. Eroding plaster combined with naturally accumulating dust to create a new layer of earth. Plants sprang up and held the soil in place, while their roots gradually destroyed the old city walls. Trees and shrubs eventually overran the lower-lying areas.

4. Ruins in the jungle
Only the stone summits of the tallest buildings escaped the jungle's encroachment. Soil could not form a stable enough layer to support plant growth there. Small temples and shrines remained visible here and there in the jungle.

5. Villages
A few settlements continued a subsistence existence in the jungle. They retained some of the ancient language of their predecessors and made use of the same primitive tools. Completely isolated in remote regions, they had no hope of re-creating the glories of the vanished civilization.

Roots versus walls
When a building is abandoned in a jungle region, vegetation quickly overruns and destroys the structure. Climbing plants, shrubs, and finally trees take root in the initial layer of overgrowth. Roots penetrate any cracks in the walls, and with time and the forest's humidity grow ever more dense. The structure's stone blocks are detached from one another, and little by little, the least resistant parts of the building collapse. Roots penetrate the foundation as well, to undermine the entire structure. Layers of sediment that accumulate next to the walls promote additional plant growth, which leads to even greater destruction.

arose on the Atlantic coast of the Yucatán Peninsula, giving birth to new societies. The cities of the deep jungle lost their importance. Some Mayan centers, especially those in the northern Yucatán, overcame the crises and absorbed the influences of such new societies as the Toltecs'. A few cities of the interior also succeeded in surviving the crises, but Uaxacmal was not among them.

With limited technology, the Mayas of Uaxacmal had achieved much and created an important civilization. But their Stone Age tools could not meet the challenge of new historical conditions and technologies. Only their complex social structure had allowed them to organize and temporarily conquer the jungle. The society that managed to impose its will on that hostile environment proved in time extremely fragile and unable to adapt to changing conditions. When the state, the entity that maintained order and guaranteed the society's smooth operation, became factionalized with internal struggles, the collective approach that assured survival in the jungle environment fragmented as well, and the civilization crumbled.

In the midst of the crises, some priests ordered the faithful to flee north to new lands. In a few years, Uaxacmal's population shrank to nothing. The city was completely abandoned, and the jungle once again held dominion over the region and its scattered human inhabitants. A few small farming settlements remained on the banks of the Xunantun. For centuries, these would maintain a primitive way of life based on a subsistence economy that had no place for kings, merchants, or priests.

The memory of Uaxacmal's glory faded. As the jungle regained control of its dominion, it quickly hid the abandoned ruins of the society that had dared to defy it.

Monument turns to hill

With the passage of time, many of the outstanding pyramids erected by the Mayas became little more to the unsuspecting eye than overgrown hills rising unexpectedly in the deep jungle. The camouflaging was a gradual process that took centuries to complete.

① Construction of a small Mayan temple-pyramid. Third century B.C.

② Enlargement of the temple with the superimposition of a new pyramid. Seventh century A.D.

③ Additional enlargement. Ninth century.

④ Abandonment of the religious center in which the pyramid stood. In the course of a few years, portions of the stucco surface deteriorated and flaked off. The jungle's torrential rains aided the process of deterioration, and the rubble that accumulated in junctures of the great steps attracted deposits of dust. Small plants sprang up, and their roots helped to fix the soil in place. Late ninth century.

⑤ Increasingly high layers of soil accumulated on the pyramid's lower sections. Shrubs grew, and eventually climbing plants and dense undergrowth surrounded the ancient structure. The accumulation of earth and plants buried the huge steps. Roots wore away the pyramid's surface and, as the decorative work crumbled, penetrated the structure's interior, helping to create soil capable of supporting even larger shrubs. Eleventh century.

⑥ The pyramid stood in ruins while a great deal of earth covered its base and steps. Tall trees grew on its sloping surfaces. Only a few stones at the summit hinted that beneath this overgrown hill stood a manmade structure. Thirteenth century.

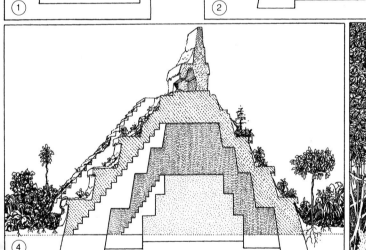

7. Strangers in the Jungle: Mid-17th Century

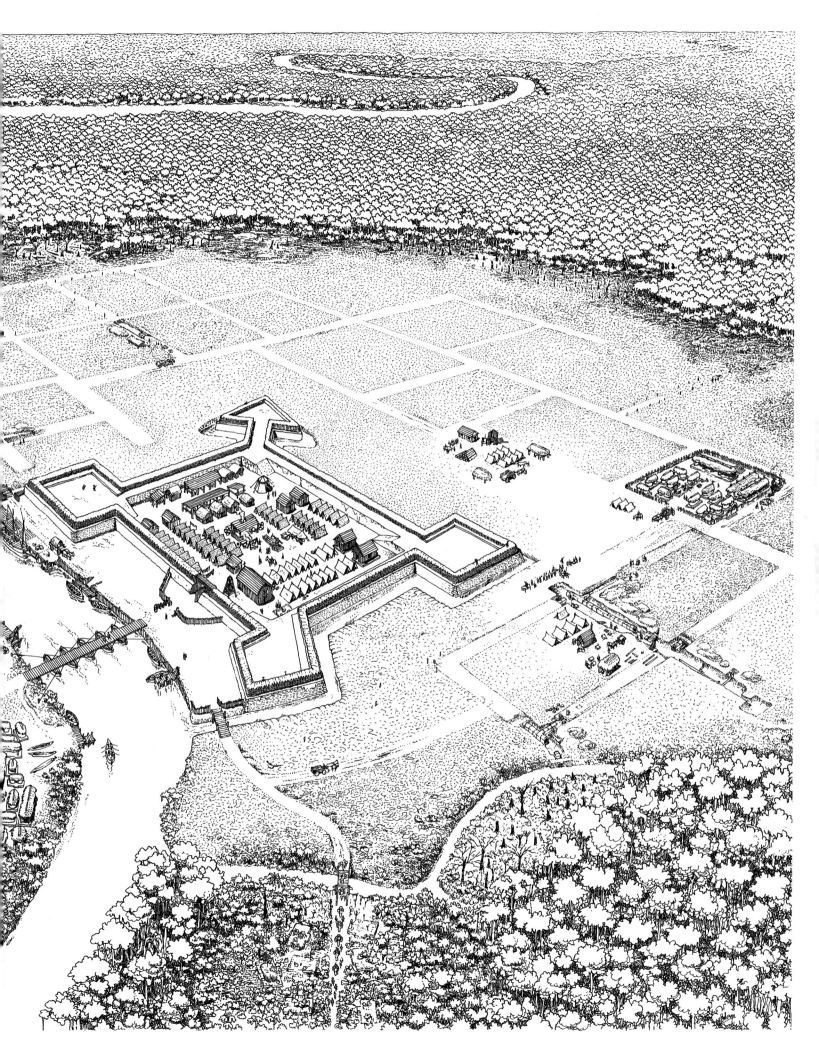

31

7. Strangers in the Jungle
Mid-17th Century

After the abandonment of Uaxacmal, life in the Xunantun jungle slipped into a routine of quiet monotony. During the first half of the sixteenth century several Spanish military expeditions ventured into the region, but all returned to Spain. The humidity, impenetrable vegetation, treacherous rivers, and poisonous creatures, along with the seeming lack of riches, discouraged the first conquistadors from staying. During the second half of the century, additional expeditions crossed the region, only to abandon it as quickly as the earlier ones had.

Around the middle of the seventeenth century, circumstances changed. The Spanish were firmly established in Guatemala and in several areas of the Yucatán. The viceroy of New Spain—later Mexico—and the captain general of Guatemala agreed to extend their authority over

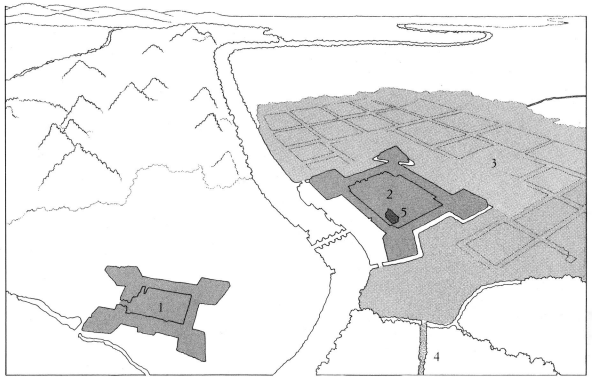

1. Fortress
During the sixteenth, seventeenth, and eighteenth centuries, European explorers in the Americas built fortifications based on European models. Temporary structures eventually were replaced by solid stone forts surrounded by trenches and flanked by bastions for artillery emplacements.

2. Military camp
Military encampments were protected from surprise attacks by field fortifications. Within the camp, huts to lodge the troops were built of logs and roofed with palm leaves. Campaign tents were also used as shelters. As soon as possible, these were replaced by more solid structures.

3. Leveling the land
Europeans in general and the Spanish in particular were free to create entirely new cities in the Americas. Unimpeded by pre-existing structures, they were able to create practical, planned cities based on a rectilinear pattern. Forested lands were cleared and leveled. Streets were laid out, and drainage tunnels were dug.

4. Trochas
Clearing tracks through the jungle was time-consuming and labor-intensive work. As a result, river transport became the prac- tical alternative to overland travel. Trochas, *or temporary jungle paths, were for many years the only land routes available.*

5. Chapel
The Spanish conquistadors were Roman Catholics, and religion played a significant role in the process of colonization. Priests always accompanied military expeditions, and every encampment included a chapel.

Jungle paths
The only way to create tracks in the jungle was to clear *trochas* with machetes. A *trocha* was a path wide enough to permit people and heavily laden pack mules to pass. It was impossible to create tracks broad enough to accommodate carts. Little-used paths were quickly reclaimed by the luxuriant vegetation.

the region between the Yucatán Peninsula and Guatemala's high plateau.

The Spaniards selected strategically located sites for the construction of cities, from which they would colonize and control the territory. The environs of the ancient center of Uaxacmal once more came to life. The Spanish established an enclave there, from which to oversee the entire Xunantun basin. Although land communications were difficult, the Xunantun was deep enough to accommodate river brigantines. A large military detachment arrived. Work began on an encampment and a fortress. Makeshift building materials were soon replaced with stone blocks scavenged from the Mayan ruins.

The fortress was designed to consolidate the Spaniards' military con-

trol of the territory, while it served as the pivotal point of their projected trade routes through the region. It was also intended to prevent British expeditions from penetrating the Xunantun interior. The British had firmly established themselves on the island of Jamaica, and from that base their privateers continually assaulted the Yucatán coasts. They eventually controlled the territories of Belize and the peninsula, and although it was impossible to drive them out, the Spaniards could at least thwart their attempts to advance through the jungle.

Soon the first colonists and Catholic clerics joined the soldiers. The captain general of Guatemala ordered construction of a genuine city. A large jungle tract was cleared and urban planning began.

Feathers versus steel

The Spanish soldiers were heavily armed. Their equipment typically included breastplate, helmet, double-edged sword, pike, and arquebus or musket, as well as heavy boots and leather clothes. Horses played an important role in the conquest of the Americas. Although they could not maneuver well in the dense jungle, the mere sight of these previously unknown animals was enough to frighten the indigenous peoples. In spite of their horses and weaponry, the Spaniards were not successful in every encounter. Although the Indians had only projectiles and stone hatchets with which to oppose the conquistadors, the jungle itself was their potent ally.

② ①

③

Encampment

Field defenses consisted of embankments, fascines (bundled branches), and palisades. Whenever possible, these were replaced by more solid fortifications.

① Earthen wall reinforced with fascines
② Wooden barracks for officers
③ Cavalry soldiers' quarters and stables
④ Infantry tent
⑤ Cooking area

④ ⑤

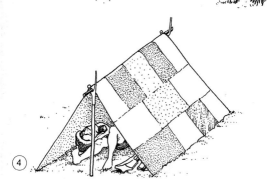

33

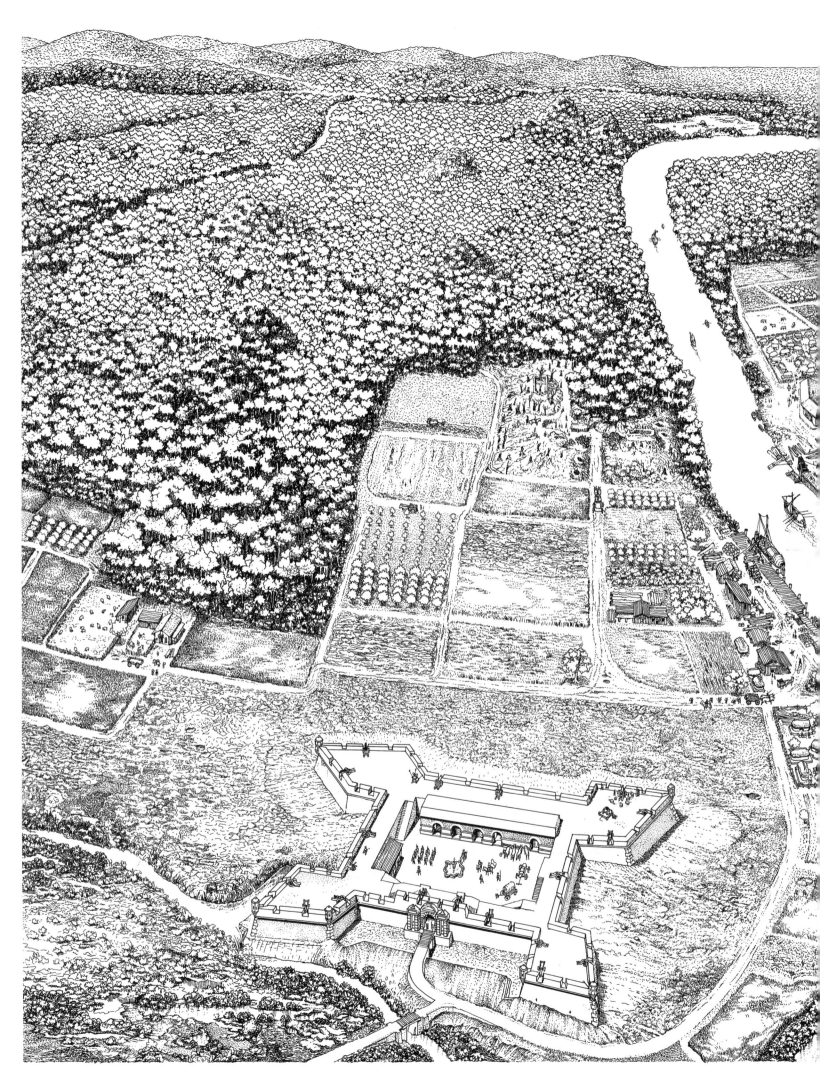

8. Birth of a Colonial City: Early 18th Century

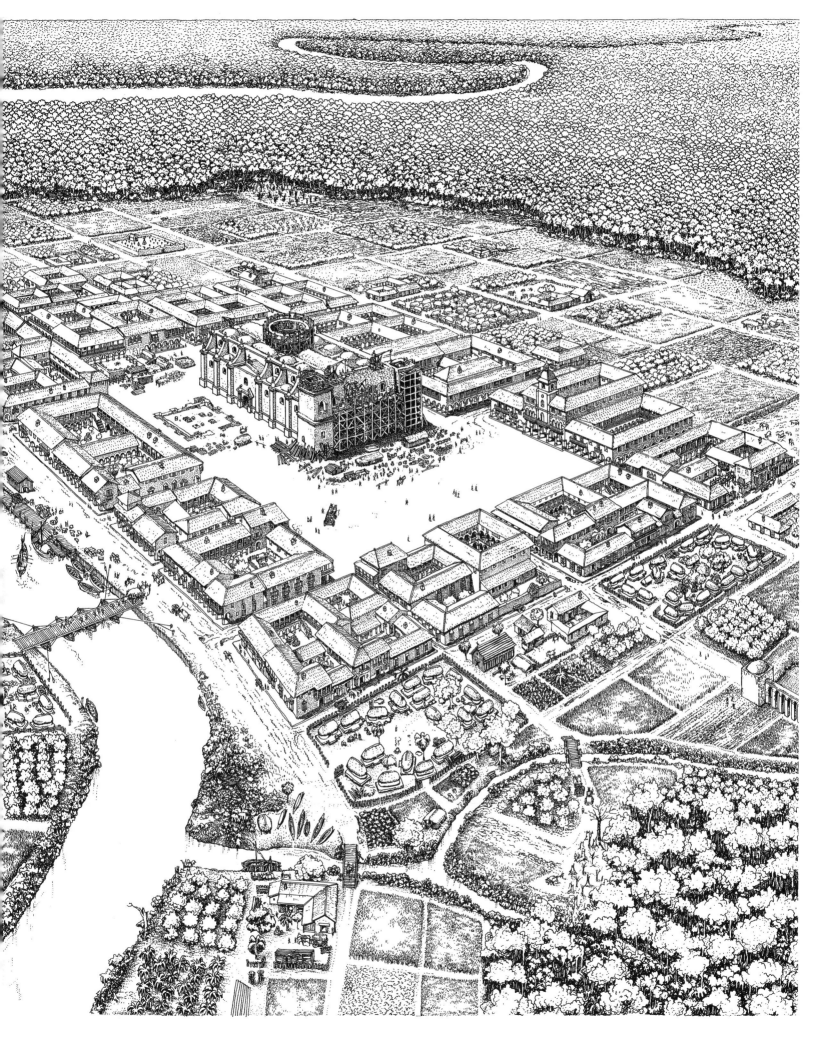

8. Birth of a Colonial City
Early 18th Century

The construction of a city in the jungle posed major problems. The Spaniards expended enormous effort not only to transform the landscape but to subdue the indigenous Indians. In contrast to Central American Indians elsewhere, who had been forced into slavery under the *encomienda* system decades earlier, the peoples native to the Xunantun Valley were relatively fortunate. They became a permanent underclass and were employed as laborers on the rapidly multiplying colonial plantations. The clergy of several religious orders assumed the task of converting them to Christianity.

The government relocated Spaniards, Creoles—people of Spanish heritage born in the Americas—and *mestizos*, people of mixed European and Indian heritage, to build and inhabit the city. Construc-

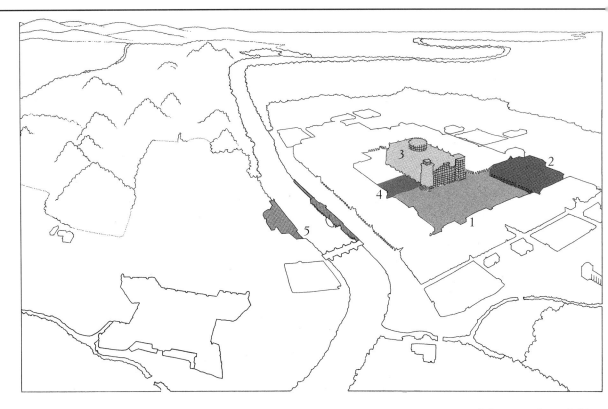

1. Central plaza or parade ground
A colonial city's central plaza formed the hub around which all other urban spaces were organized. Such principal public buildings as churches, palaces, and hospitals were generally situated on the plaza that also served as a market- and meeting place. Plazas were required to have porticoes and to be of sufficient size to accommodate festivals, including exhibitions of horsemanship. Their design was based on those of Castile in Spain, which had taken as their models ancient Roman forums.

2. Governor's palace
During a colonial city's initial development, military authorities controlled both civil and military matters. Military governors reported to the captains general and viceroys, who were responsible for more extensive territories. The tribunal, in collaboration with the governor, was charged with administering justice. Splendid palaces were built to house the governor's family and offices.

3. Cathedral under construction
The cathedral was the principal church of a Roman Catholic diocese and served as the bishop's seat and the canonical capital. The organization of a diocese, as well as plans for a new cathedral, required direct authorization by the pope. The Spanish initiated work on a number of cathedrals in Central America.

4. Courtyard of the Indians
A chapel annexed to the cathe-dral and opening onto an extensive courtyard served as a site for open-air services during religious festivals. These services were intended to convert the Indian population to Roman Catholicism.

5. Wharves
The dense tropical jungle made river travel the most dependable form of communication and transport. Cities set up small ports where brigantines and barges could moor. Numerous buildings were erected to serve as storehouses for arriving mer-chandise and commodities awaiting shipment.

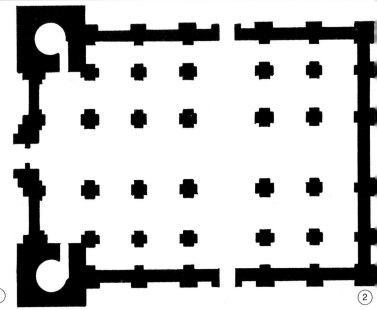

tion of the first residential areas soon began. Spanish colonial cities followed urban planning laws established during the reign of Philip II. These set up a grid pattern extending from a central plaza, or square.

In Xunantun, the central plaza was a large parade ground presided over by a baroque palace that served as the governor's residence and also housed the colonial government bureaucracy. Of greater symbolic importance, however, was the spectacular cathedral, which was begun in the final decades of the seventeenth century. This monumental stone mass was dedicated to San Rafael, or Saint Raphael, and even in its incomplete state it towered as the central reference point of the city and its surroundings.

Near the cathedral and at an angle to the plaza, residences for the church hierarchy and a small hospital were constructed. An enclosure known as the Courtyard of the Indians was used for preaching to the indigenous peoples, who regularly gathered in the city. Although presided over by European priests, these religious meetings vaguely recalled those that had been held centuries earlier around the pyramids of Uaxacmal.

The infant city adopted the name San Rafael, and was also known as San Rafael de Xunantun. The early conquistadors had been convinced that the Catholic saint protected and assisted them in their initial period of occupation.

The river and a small port served as the city's link to other settlements and the coast. Land communications remained unsatisfactory, despite continuing efforts to transform the jungle paths into viable roads.

Construction techniques
The Spanish in Central America used many of the construction techniques employed in European Renaissance and baroque structures, especially vaults and cupolas to roof interior areas. Stone, brick, plaster, and stucco were common building materials.

Building a cathedral
Construction of a large cathedral required years of labor. Spanish architects designed the plans and supervised the project. Construction was overseen by a foreman, often a *mestizo*, who understood the rich building tradition of the early Central Americans. Stonemasons, plasterers, sculptors, and other craftsmen also were drawn from the *mestizo* or Indian populations. The resulting structures represented an impressive blend of European and Central American traditions.

① Cross section
② Plan
③ Cross section
④ Facade
⑤ Vaults
⑥ Cupola
⑦ Bell tower

9. Churches, Monasteries, Palaces: Mid-18th Century

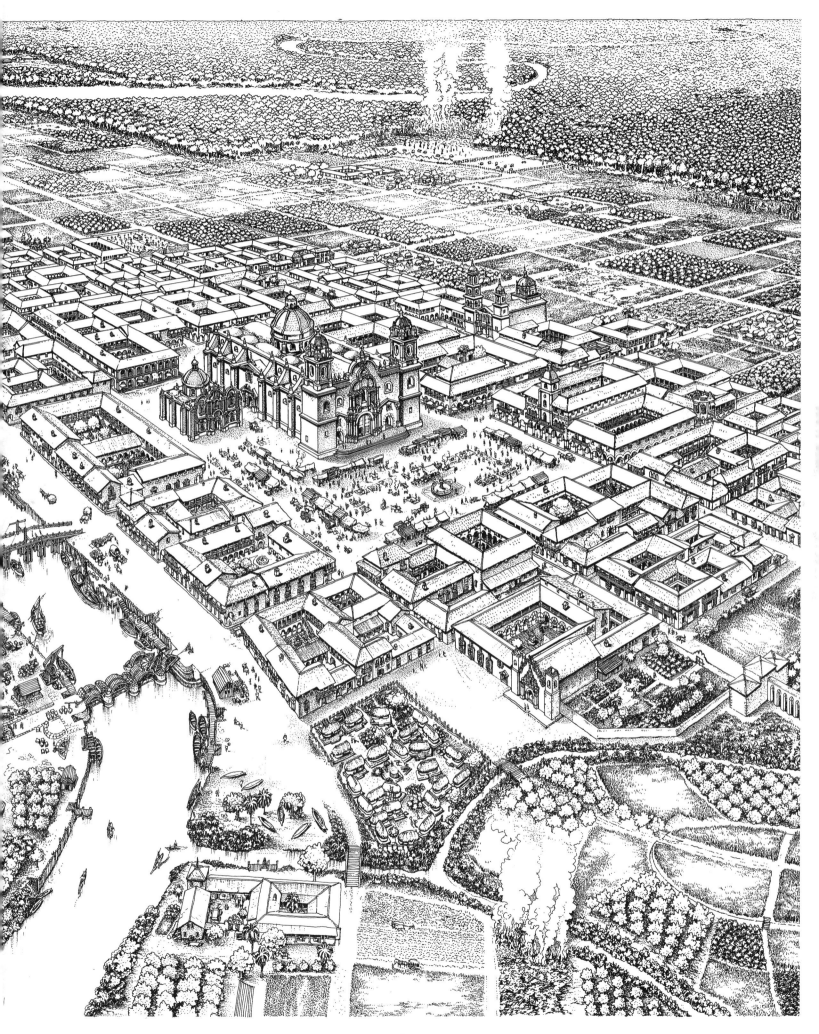

9. Churches, Monasteries, Palaces
Mid-18th Century

By the middle of the eighteenth century, San Rafael was a lively city. New residential blocks and palaces had been built. Work on the cathedral was completed, and a pair of monasteries had been built. Dozens of one-story houses with tidy interior courtyards flanked the city's broad streets. The Spanish urban planners had designed a city that could accommodate growth without becoming cramped; the major difficulty of this period was filling the broad avenues with buildings of proportionate grandeur.

Circulating in San Rafael's streets were Spaniards, Creoles, *mestizos*, Indians, and African Americans. Africans had arrived in Central America as slaves, and were forced to work as field laborers or house servants for the nobility and wealthy landowners. The city functioned as a market-

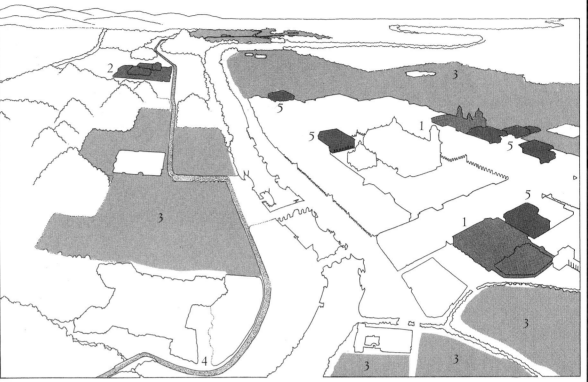

1. Monasteries
Monasteries were established in and around Central America's cities as they had been in Europe's Roman Catholic countries. These religious communities were dedicated to converting Indians to the Catholic faith. The Dominican and Franciscan orders were especially active in this work.

2. Franciscan mission
Far from the cities, in remote and isolated areas with high concentrations of Indians, missions were built to spread the Catholic faith. Each mission was a self-sufficient enclave whose clerics organized the social and working lives of the indigenous peoples.

3. Plantations
Wealthy landowners amassed vast plantations. Their fields were initially devoted to cacao and indigo production, but sugar cane and coffee later became the principal crops. Harvests were destined for the export trade. Multicrop subsistence farming, practiced for centuries by the Indians, gradually disappeared as new tracts were cleared for single-crop cultivation.

4. Highways
To improve communications, roads were built. Continual maintenance was required to keep them clear of vegetation. The most important roads were called *caminos reales, or highways.*

5. Palaces and mansions
Spanish-born nobles and wealthy Creole families built palatial residences in the city. Some also built *haciendas, or plantation houses. The architectural style of these residences was colonial baroque.*

Mission
The mission complex functioned as a small city and included a variety of services and structures. The church or chapel was the must sumptuous and significant architectural element. Other buildings stood fortress-style around a large courtyard, and a wall surrounding the complex offered some protection against attack.

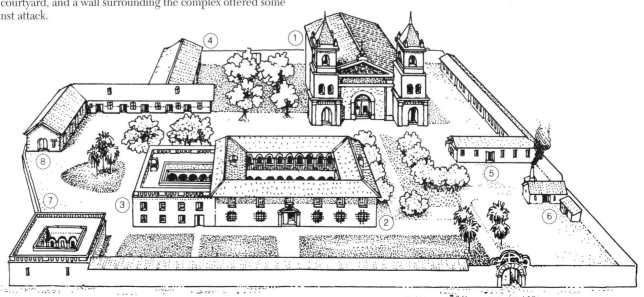

① Church
② Friars' quarters
③ School
④ Stables
⑤ Sheds
⑥ Blacksmith's workshop
⑦ Hospital/infirmary
⑧ Indians' quarters

place for the entire region, and a variety of professionals—doctors, surgeons, barbers, lawyers, merchants, coopers, pharmacists, and others—offered their services there. It was even possible to find British products in San Rafael's markets, thanks to the widely tolerated smuggling carried on by British merchants in Belize.

Land communications were notably improved by the construction of highways, along which heavily loaded carriages could safely pass. A new wooden bridge was built over the Xunantun while engineers studied the project of building a permanent stone span.

Around the city's outskirts, the jungle retreated as new tracts were cleared for cultivation. Large plantations controlled by wealthy landowners and devoted to the cash crops of cacao and indigo steadily increased in number.

Franciscan friars redoubled their efforts to convert the local Indians. Several missions were established in the Xunantun basin, one very close to San Rafael. The Franciscans offered the Indians work and spiritual instruction, and the new skills and technologies they taught spread throughout the entire Indian community.

The apparent harmony of everyday life, however, hid deep conflicts that would explode years later. Native Spaniards kept the Creole middle class in an inferior position by retaining all positions of power for themselves. Indians, who made up a major portion of the population, were marginalized as a permanent underclass. These socioeconomic conditions created the basis for conflicts that would continue unresolved in succeeding centuries.

Palace
The palaces of colonial cities were built around a central courtyard. They were generally one or two stories tall and constructed in the colonial baroque style, which was heavily influenced by the region's indigenous architecture.

10. Echoes of the Enlightenment: Early 19th Century

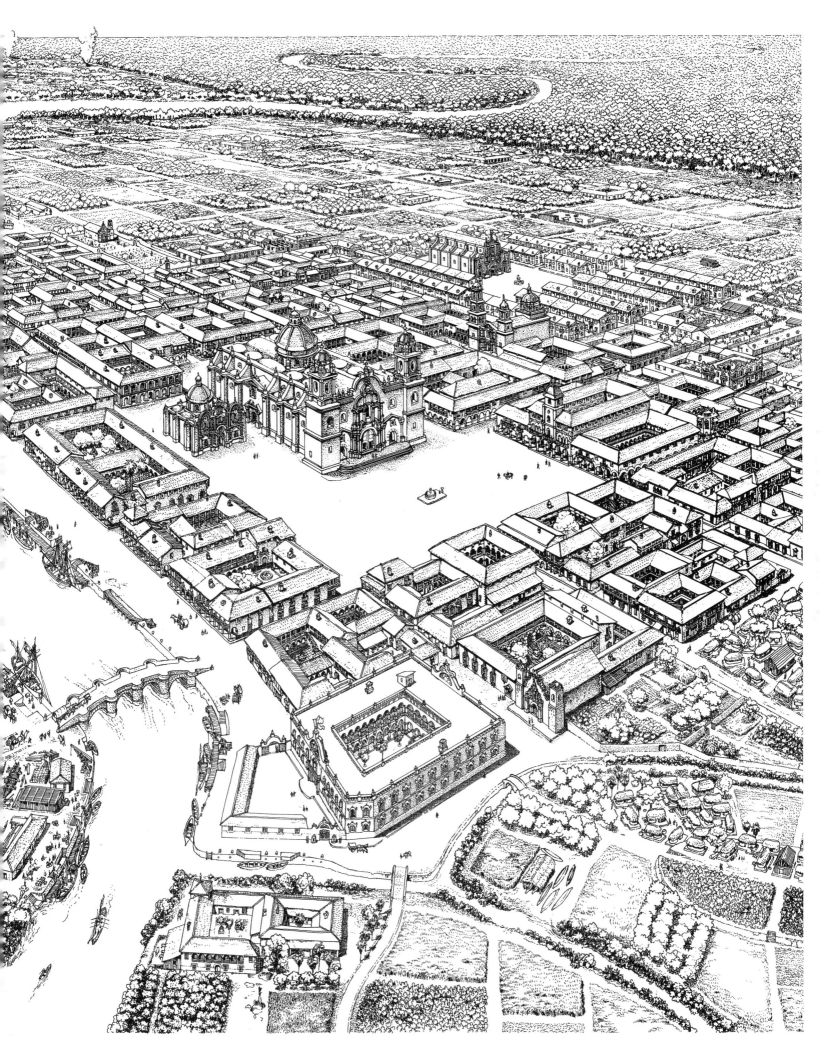

10. Echoes of the Enlightenment
Early 19th Century

San Rafael continued its slow growth. In Spain, the Bourbon dynasty assumed power and produced a succession of kings whose reigns were strongly influenced by the ideas of the Enlightenment. This philosophic movement had swept Europe in the eighteenth century and given birth to democratic movements and liberal reforms. The Spanish Bourbon kings hoped to apply some of its principles to the management of their colonies in the Americas. San Rafael and all of Spanish Central America benefited from the appointment of new, more effective administrators.

The army, newly regulated and organized, was employed on public construction projects. Barracks for an infantry regiment were built in San Rafael, and work began on improving the road system. In the final decades of the eighteenth century, construction of a major new urban

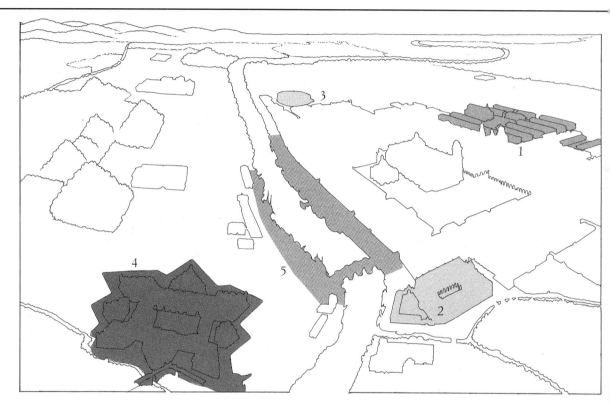

1. New district
The new districts of the late eighteenth and early nineteenth centuries were built in the neoclassical style. Roads followed a grid pattern.

2. Barracks
Enlightened monarchs sponsored a regular army loyal to the crown. City barracks were built to provide housing for troops. The army was put to work on civil engineering projects.

3. Plaza de toros
Spain exported to Spanish America the tradition of bullfighting. At first bullfights were held in the central plazas of colonial cities. Later, permanent plazas de toros, or bull rings, were built. The plazas were similar to ancient Roman amphitheaters.

4. Fortifications
On five continents, the colonial powers remodeled old fortifications or erected new ones using the technologies perfected by the great French engineer Vauban.

These fortifications were potent reminders of Spain's power and served to safeguard colonial territories as much from internal threats as from external assaults.

5. Channeling the river
Military engineers undertook a variety of public works projects. They supervised the building of roads and bridges, the rechanneling of the river, and the construction of a port.

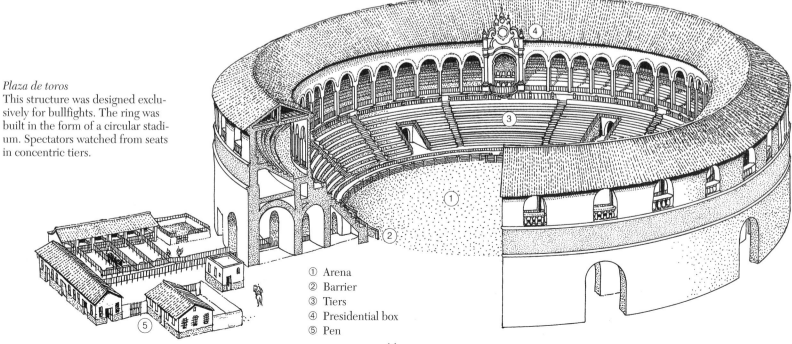

Plaza de toros
This structure was designed exclusively for bullfights. The ring was built in the form of a circular stadium. Spectators watched from seats in concentric tiers.

① Arena
② Barrier
③ Tiers
④ Presidential box
⑤ Pen

district was begun. The neighborhood of San Rafael "Chico" was built to provide living space for artisans and merchants. It followed a more practical grid pattern than that of the main city. Its streets were designed so that sunlight could reach even one-story houses. A monumental fountain anchored a central plaza dominated by a church in the Spanish neoclassical style.

The new quarter did not eliminate the slums on the city's outskirts, where the Indian underclass still lived in simple huts. The recently abandoned fortress was enlarged and restored in anticipation of possible conflicts brought on by mounting tensions between the great European powers.

A bull ring was built on the city outskirts. In the Spanish tradition, corridas de toros, or bullfights, were popular in the American colonies.

With the construction of a permanent bull ring, the number of *corridas* increased, as did the popularity of the entertainment.

The plantations that surrounded the city also benefited from innovations. Sugar cane and coffee became the most important crops.

Beneath the order that seemed to prevail in San Rafael, conflict continued to fester. The principles of liberalism that had jolted the world with the outbreak of the French Revolution began to gain popularity among San Rafael's Creole middle class. The independence won by the United States from Britain was also a stimulus to their desire for freedom from Spain. With the start of the nineteenth century, Spain was entering its final years as a Central American colonial power. The Napoleonic wars and the collapse of absolute monarchies in Europe led inevitably to the crumbling of the Spanish colonial empire.

Neoclassical residences
In the newly built neoclassical districts, houses of similar proportions and facades flanked rectilinear streets. These houses typically included a ground floor and a second story connected by an internal stairway. An indoor well furnished water. In contrast to houses of preceding centuries, not all the new dwellings included internal courtyards.

① Shop and storage area
② Kitchen
③ Living quarters
④ Well

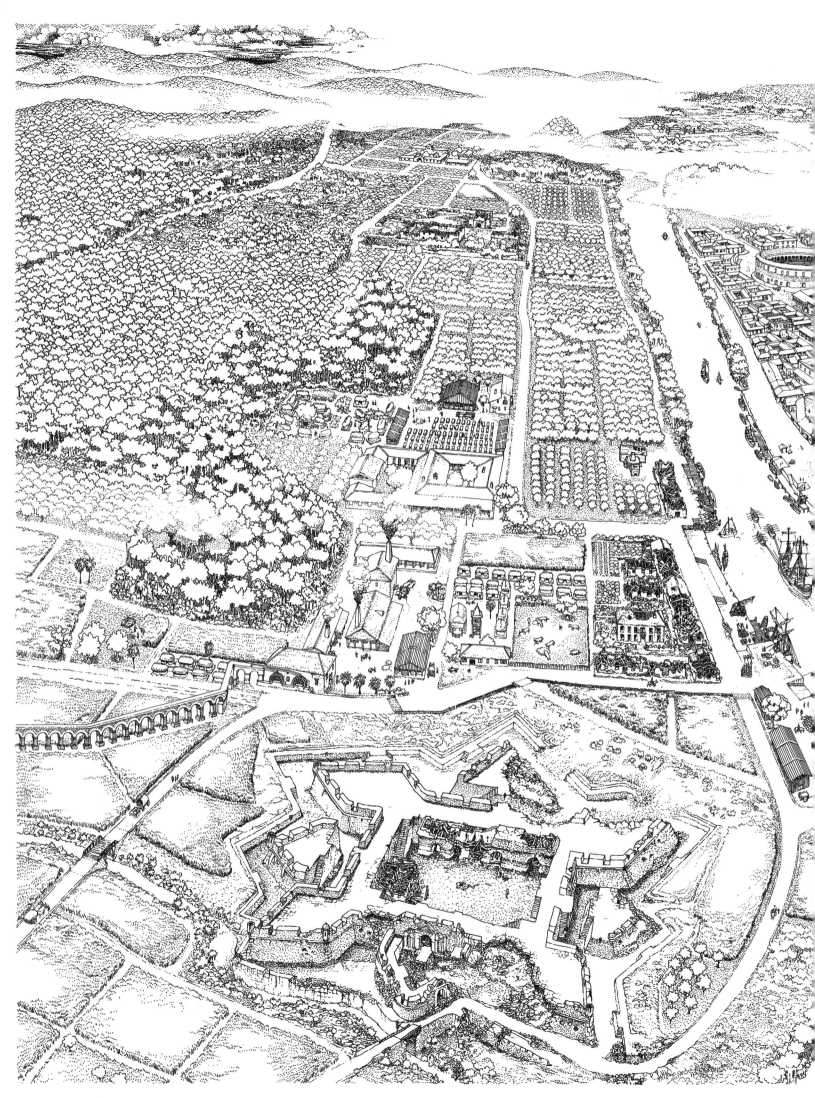

11. Crises and Dynamism: Mid-19th Century

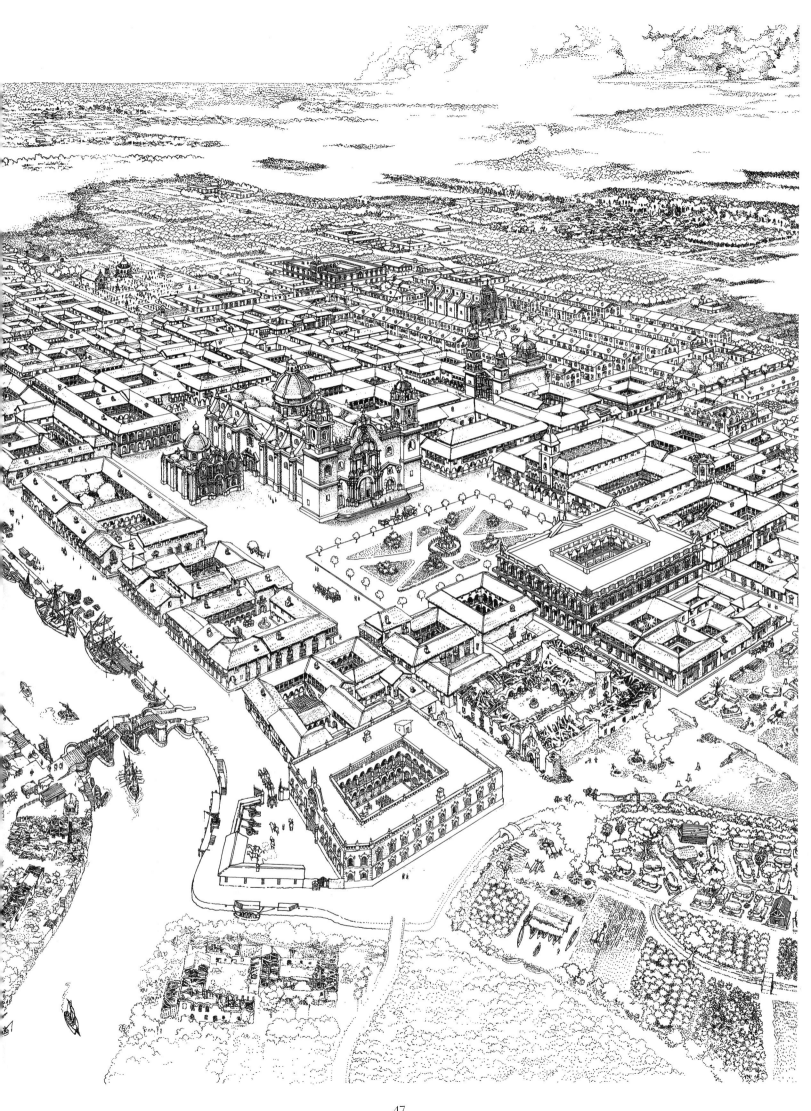

11. Crises and Dynamism
Mid-19th Century

By the mid-nineteenth century, San Rafael de Xunantun had become the district capital of a Central American republic. The preceding decades had been extremely difficult for the city. War between the royalist supporters of the colonial regime and those eager for independence had been costly and had included the destruction of many plantations. Independence was achieved in the end, but new problems arose. Political struggles continued as liberals and conservatives constantly opposed one another, not only verbally but also in military clashes. At the same time, social conflicts erupted throughout the new republic. In Xunantun, the subjugated Indians began a violent social struggle. They took control of San Rafael and burned down several city districts. From the first moments of independence, the Central American republics

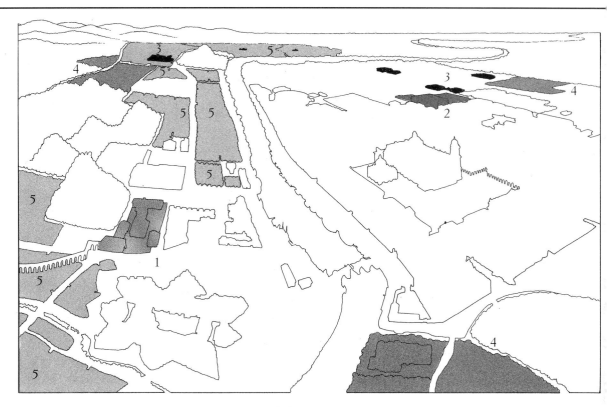

1. Sugar refinery
Special processing was required to transform raw cane into loaves of refined sugar. A mill was one of several specialized structures necessary to the complex process.

2. Tobacco factory
Tobacco leaves had to be dried before they could be turned into smoking products. The dried leaves were made into cigars by skilled workers.

3. *Haciendas*
The haciendas, *or plantation houses, of major landholders were mansions furnished with every luxury. They included laborers' lodgings, storehouses, workshops, and other outbuildings. Owners were frequently absentee landlords who made only brief visits to their haciendas.*

4. Abandoned plantations
The conflicts of the early nineteenth century accounted for a decline in agriculture in some regions. Many plantations were abandoned and only returned to productivity years later.

5. Plantations
The combined interests of landowners and foreign importers led to the predominance of specific crops. Sugar cane, coffee, and tobacco held places of primary importance in the republic's economy. Single cash-crop production resulted in the phasing out of traditional subsistence farming.

Sugar refinery
The processing of sugar from cane was a major Central American industry. In the mid-nineteenth century, modern plants had not yet been built, and the industry continued to operate by traditional methods. The cane was ground in horse- or water-powered mills. The liquid sugar obtained was channeled into boilers, where it was cooked down to a syrup. The syrup flowed into graduated filtering receptacles, the lowest of which collected residual liquid while the uppermost retained the crystallized sugar. The resulting sugar loaves were oven dried. The quality of the sugar could be improved by repeating the refining process.

① Hydraulic mill for grinding cane
② Boilers
③ Syrup in filtering receptacles
④ Drying sugar loaves

exhibited the social and political instability that would remain a constant in decades to follow.

The city shared the period's hardships. Many buildings were destroyed in the conflict. Following the passage of anticlerical measures by new governments, some monasteries were abandoned or burned. San Rafael not only ceased to grow, its population dramatically decreased.

Political decline was accompanied by economic stagnation. The plantations lowered their rates of production; some temporarily shut down. In spite of the disasters, the agricultural industry slowly recovered. Once the Spanish colonial administration fell, British and American merchants hastened to increase their economic influence in the region. Demand from foreign markets accounted for a continuous increase in the amount of acreage devoted to sugar cane, coffee, and tobacco cultivation.

By the mid-nineteenth century, San Rafael had recovered from its war damage. Devastated buildings were cleared, and the city entered a new phase of development. The republican government commissioned an impressive administration building to house district authorities. A large sugar refinery financed by foreign investors and a tobacco factory were two other additions to the urban landscape during this period.

A number of plantations in the city's outlying areas managed to resume production. Some owners built private refineries to process their sugar cane. The river continued to be the principal artery of communication with the outside world. Goods from the Xunantun basin traveled by barge to the major coastal ports.

49

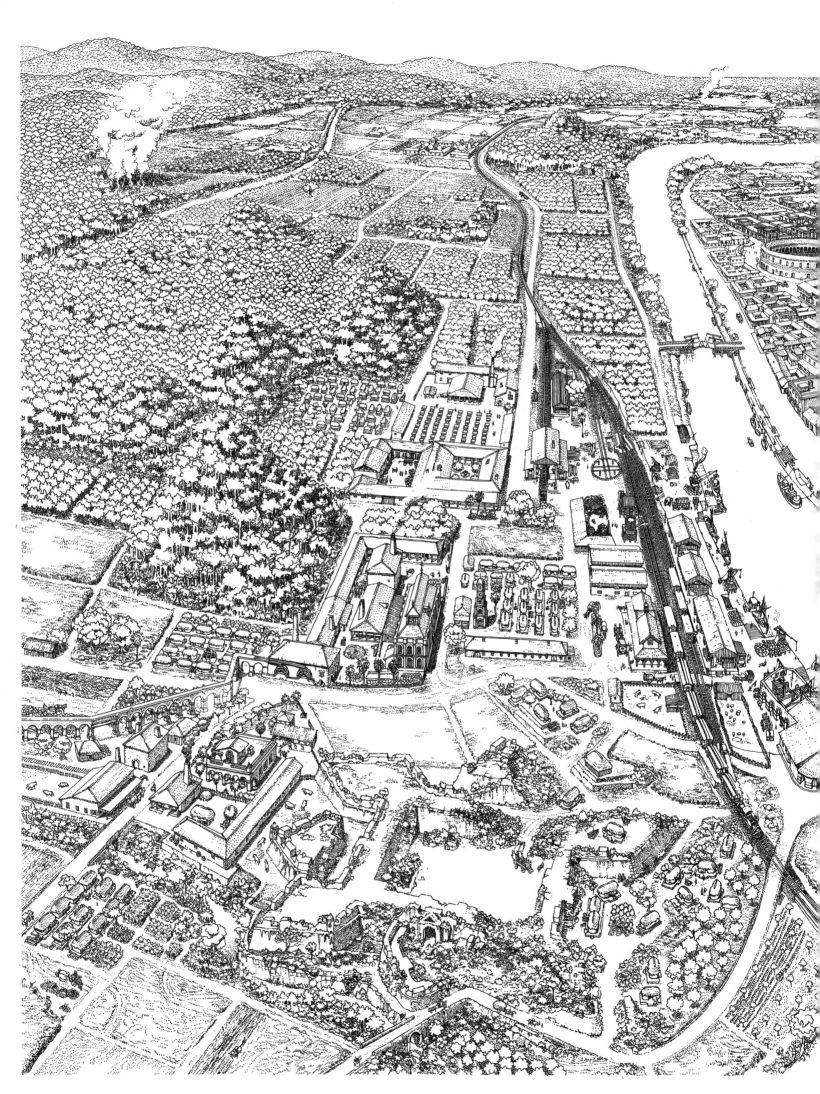

12. New Colonialism: International Fruit Companies: Early 20th Century

12. New Colonialism: International Fruit Companies

Early 20th Century

The major scientific and technical advances of the first industrial revolution in Europe and North America did not affect Central America until much later. Only in the early twentieth century did San Rafael de Xunantun's urban landscape begin to reflect innovations that had been commonplace for decades in industrialized nations. Among these were railroads, steamboats, steam-powered factories, and a rudimentary streetcar system.

At the close of the nineteenth century, North American fruit companies established bases in the Xunantun region. General Fruit Company and the Sugar, Cocoa, & Coffee Company were joined in the twentieth century by a chewing gum manufacturer, Atlantic-Pacific Gum.

The fruit companies bought vast tracts of land for development. They

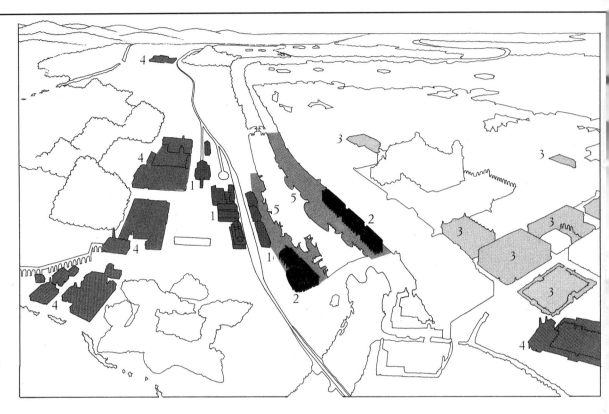

1. Railroad station and train services
The railroads were used primarily for transporting commodities. Stations were equipped with repair shops, warehouses, and sheds. They also included reserves of coal and elevated water tanks to resupply locomotives.

2. Warehouses and depots
Raw materials were stored in warehouses near the port or the railroad station. These depositories were also used to store food and other merchandise shipped to the city for sale in its markets.

3. Service centers
Economic development brought new services. These included postal and telegraph offices, banks, and branch offices of trade and insurance companies.

4. Processing plants
Some raw materials destined for export were partially processed before shipping. Final processing and packaging occurred abroad, in the plants of the foreign-owned companies.

5. Docks
The development of steamboat traffic on the river made renovation of the port necessary. Warehouses and depositories rose in the vicinity of the docks. These held commodities awaiting shipment and reserves of coal to power both boats and factories.

Cacao processing
Beyond having significant nutritional value, cacao was and is the essential ingredient of chocolate. To obtain cocoa paste, workers treated the seed pods to a ten-day fermentation process. The acidic and sugar-rich pulp covering each seed assisted fermentation. The fermented seeds were dried and lightly roasted. As a final step, they were milled to fine powder.

① Cacao harvesting
② Fermentation warehouse
③ Shelling fermented seed pods
④ Drying racks

also leased land from major property owners or contracted for those owners to raise and sell specific fruit crops to them. As a consequence of this system, land was distributed even more unjustly than before: a few powerful citizens and three foreign companies owned nearly all the republic's acreage. The native peoples who worked the vast plantations as farmhands were allowed only a few small plots in which to raise vegetables, grain, and fruit for survival.

Both General Fruit and the Sugar, Cocoa, & Coffee Company built depots, warehouses, and offices in San Rafael. From there they directed their agrarian empires. The city port was busy with steamships taking on cargos of bananas, coffee, cacao, sugar, and *chicle*, the chewing gum base, to transport downriver. Large vessels—some refrigerated—waited there to take on produce and transport it to foreign markets. Modern sugar refineries and coffee-drying houses were built on the city's out-skirts, and new working-class districts sprang up to house the fruit companies' native-born employees.

An iron bridge was built over the Xunantun to connect the river's banks permanently. Its construction encouraged new urban growth on the left, or far, bank.

As a result of its economic power, General Fruit Company had enormous influence on the republic's government. The company obtained a concession for one of its subsidiaries to operate a railroad line, Central American Railways. Track was laid along the left bank of the Xunantun, from the coast as far as San Rafael. There it split into branch lines that served the fruit company's more remote holdings. The North American company's acquisition of this vital transportation and communications link gave it control of the trade and made it the true boss of the Xunantun basin.

Railroad station
The railroad station complex was primarily devoted to the shipment of commodities.

① Main depot with control room, ticket window, and passenger waiting room
② Warehouses
③ Sheds for loading and unloading goods
④ Raised water tank for suppling locomotives

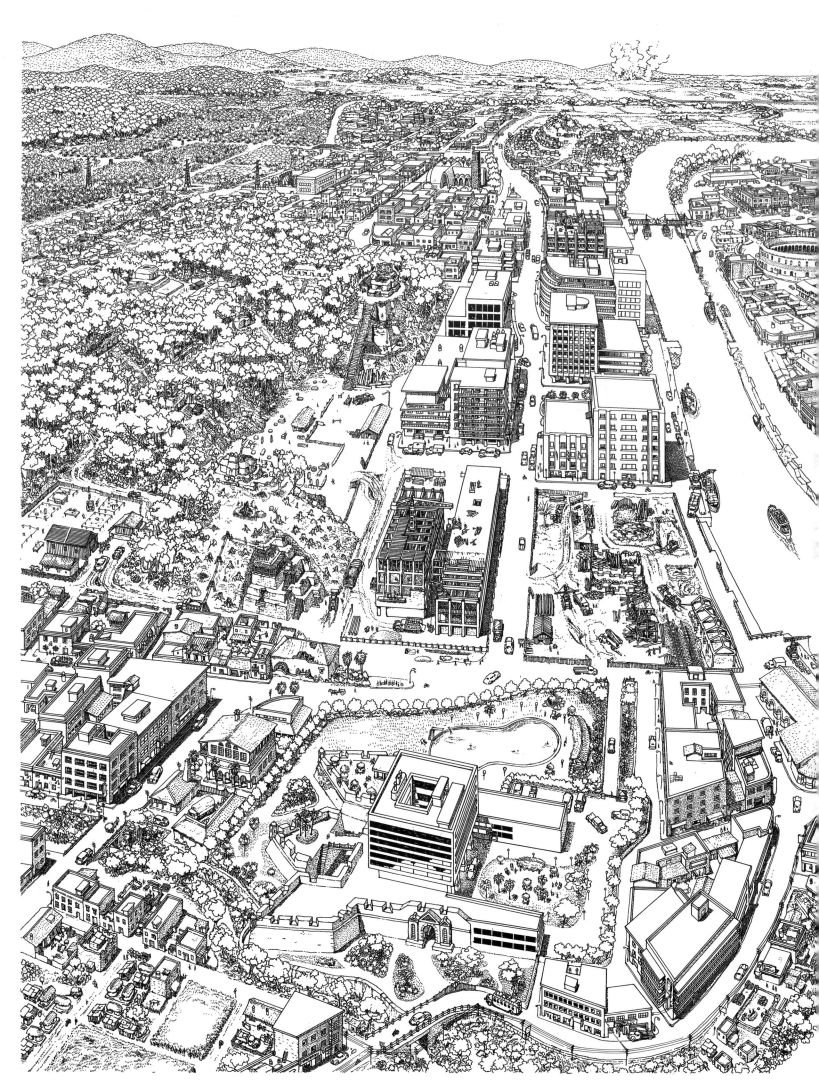

13. Impressive Growth: Mid-20th Century

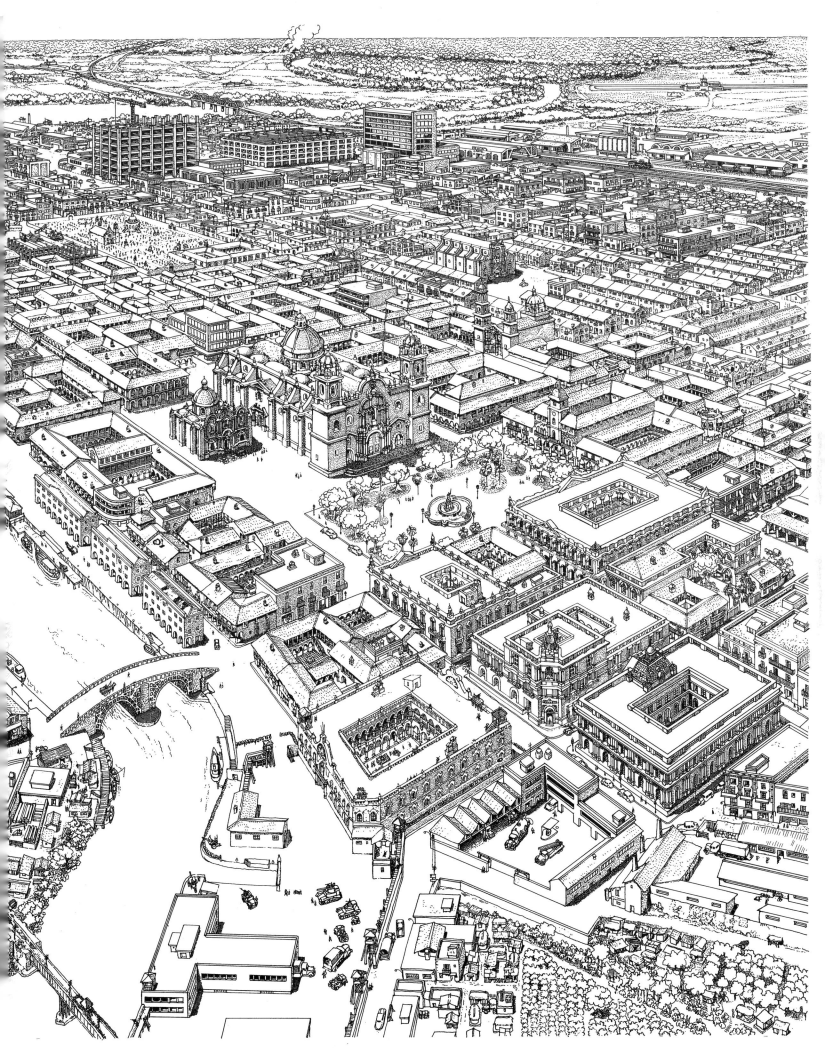

13. Impressive Growth
Mid-20th Century

Many factors were responsible for San Rafael's extraordinary mid-century growth. The infant mortality rate decreased sharply as a result of advances in medicine and improvements in sanitation. At the same time, life expectancy increased in the region. A population explosion that would continue throughout the century began. Poor people from the republic's other districts moved to the Xunantun basin in the hope of creating better lives in the still developing region. These newcomers cleared remote areas and established settlements. Meanwhile, landholders extended the reach of their plantations. As a result, the once impenetrable jungle of the Xunantun was in retreat. The leafy forests became a memory that survived only in the minds of the region's oldest inhabitants.

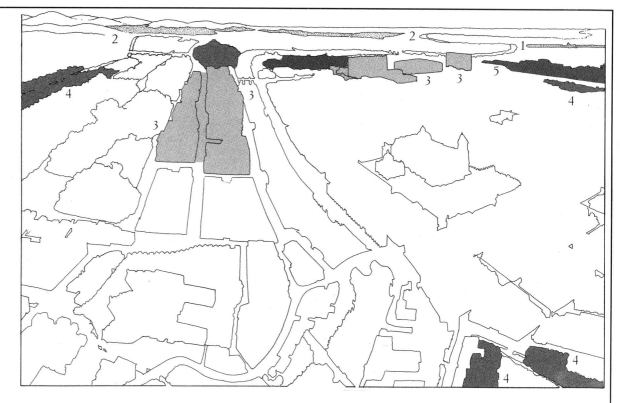

1. Airport
Civil aviation developed rapidly after World War II. Planes of increasing capacity were able to carry passengers and freight to distant destinations quickly.

2. Deforestation
The expansion of agricultural and livestock industries and of timber interests resulted in the progressive disappearance of the tropical forests. The loss of the jungle upset both the ecological balance and the climate of the region.

3. New city center
Concentrated in the new urban downtowns were service industries, professional offices, stores, restaurants, movie theaters, and other fixtures of modern urban life.

4. Outlying districts
Families and individuals who migrated to the city in search of work set up makeshift shelters on the city's outskirts. The population explosion increased their numbers, as did a steady influx of peasants, driven from farmlands by the loss of fields to industry.

5. Industrial zones
Agricultural processing plants continued to occupy an important place in the urban landscape.

Urban ambiance
The majority of mid-twentieth-century Central American cities were studies in contrasts. New buildings stood side by side with colonial palaces. Signs of every description advertised a wide variety of services. A large proportion of the population was transient. Native peoples rubbed shoulders with *mestizos* and with transplanted Europeans, to form an ever-changing human mosaic.

Masses of immigrants settled in San Rafael itself, further increasing the city's burgeoning population. On the city's outskirts lay poor districts made up of hundreds of families, who often lacked the means even to feed themselves.

Major renewal projects were undertaken to create a new city center near the ancient walls. These included construction of a new hospital, government office buildings, and a university center for anthropological studies. Other structures previously unknown in San Rafael began to appear, scattered throughout the city: public schools, fire stations, a soccer stadium, and, on the outskirts, a few light industrial plants, marking increased industrialization.

San Rafael continued as chief marketplace and service center for the surrounding region. Its role as the nucleus of a vigorous agricultural region continued, and the giant foreign companies maintained their positions of power. The modernization of the railroad, in conjunction with the construction of new highways and a small airport, markedly improved communications with the rest of the country.

Nearby hydroelectric plants furnished the city with electrical power. With the assistance of some foreign universities, local authorities began to excavate the ancient Mayan religious center. As systematic digs brought to light the antique ruins, the past began to share space with a rapidly changing present.

Soccer stadium
During the twentieth century, soccer became the most popular spectator sport in Latin America. Most major cities built soccer stadiums, and some of these structures incorporated the most up-to-date design and engineering technologies.

① Field
② Premium seats
③ Reserved seats
④ Grandstands
⑤ Scoreboard
⑥ Cross-section of support structure
⑦ Steel supports for dome
⑧ Access ways

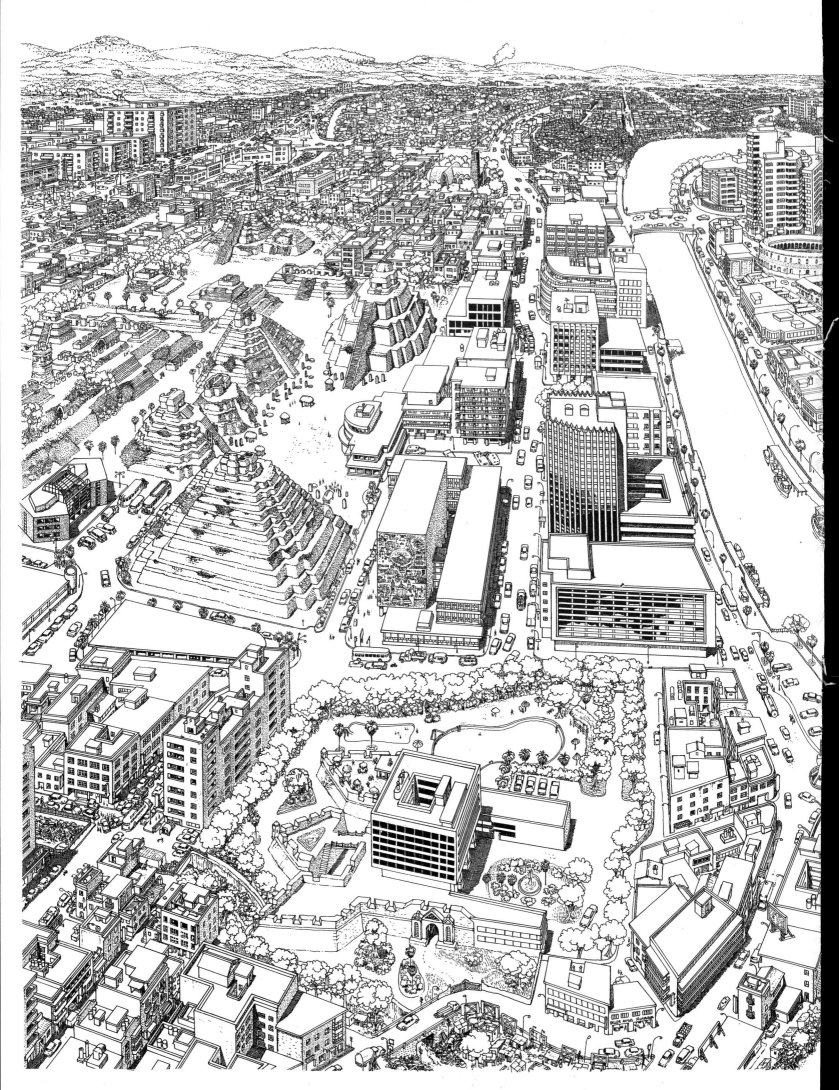

14. Unchecked Expansion: Uncertain Future: Late 20th Century

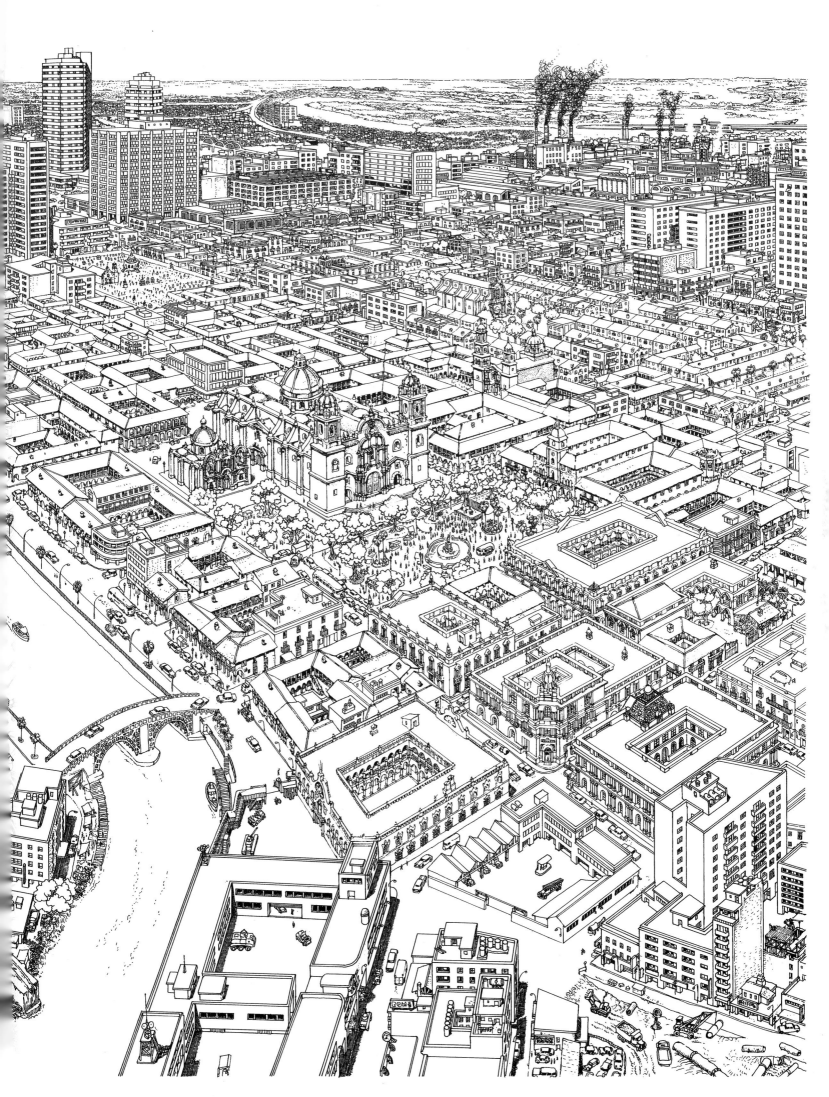

14. Unchecked Expansion; Uncertain Future

Late 20th Century

San Rafael's mid-twentieth-century urban explosion continued uncontrolled throughout the following decades. Hoards of impoverished people settled in the constantly expanding slums on the city's periphery. These districts, where thousands of huts, shacks, and other makeshift dwellings formed chaotic settlements, lacked all infrastructure and services.

The city center, with its stunning new buildings and prosperous residential districts, stood in sharp contrast, making the gap between rich and poor brutally evident. A small and relatively powerless middle class could do little to balance the city's inequities.

Growth increased the atmosphere of conflict that had smoldered for decades because of social inequities and political instability. San Rafael

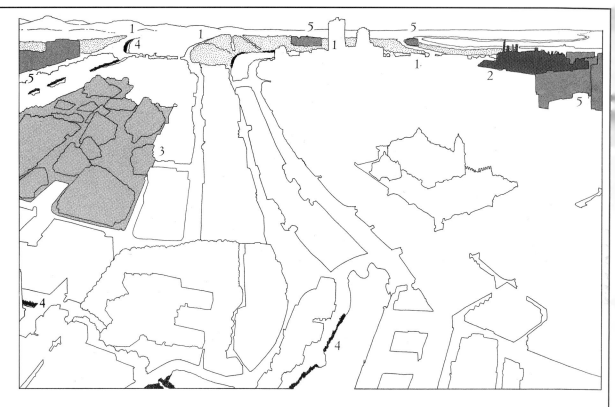

1. City outskirts
Makeshift slums sprang up on the city's outskirts. These districts reflected both the population explosion and the region's social inequities. They were typical of most cities in economically underdeveloped countries.

2. Industrial parks
Efforts at industrialization were made in many Central American cities. The results were generally not sufficient to allow the countries to achieve industrial or postindustrial societies.

3. Archaeological park
The restoration and preservation of the city's heritage was an expensive project to finance. Administrators turned to international organizations and foreign universities for assistance. Money invested in restoring the ancient ruins was recovered, with a profit, through tourist revenues.

4. Garbage dumps
The elimination of wastes was always a problem in cities lacking well-developed infrastructures. *Unregulated dumping frequently occurred, creating areas that posed health risks.*

5. Housing projects
Housing projects were built to improve the situation of the city's poorest inhabitants, but could not provide space for even a reasonable percentage of an urban population whose numbers continued to grow.

Huts and makeshift dwellings
In some areas, especially in the region's traditional agricultural centers, Mayan-style huts continued to be built. These varied only slightly from those built centuries before. Where possible, several huts were built around a small garden plot.

The increasing shortage of materials once abundant in the jungle—hardwoods for beams and vegetation for roofing—made this type of comfortable hut increasingly difficult and expensive to build. In addition, the huts' rounded angles were ill suited to manufactured furniture. As a result, traditional huts were gradually replaced by rectangular, stone-rubble dwellings with dirt floors.

In the poorest and most marginalized districts of the large cities, any material at hand was used to construct lean-tos and shacks.

① Traditional Mayan-style hut
② Rubble-work hut
③ Makeshift shack

de Xunantun's leading characteristics at the close of the twentieth century were expansion and deepening social divisions. The continuing population explosion raised fears for the future.

Efforts to redevelop and modernize the city continued, but such efforts were of necessity inadequate to the scope of the problems. The city center with its government offices, company headquarters, shops, and services, was again rebuilt. Housing projects were created to provide an alternative to makeshift slums. Efforts were made to extend electric power, running water, and the city sewage system to as many districts as possible. The few nearby areas that had escaped deforestation were protected and turned into parks.

The remains of the Mayan religious center of Uaxacmal were excavated and restored. An archaeological district was established, and several hotels were built in an effort to attract tourists and their revenues. A large new airport was built at some distance from the greater metropolitan area.

In a new industrial park, a few plants struggled to launch an era of industrial development in the Xunantun.

San Rafael prepared to meet the twenty-first century, as did the cities of other emerging nations, with a multitude of unsolved problems.

Landmark: University library
Buildings erected through public initiatives or under the sponsorship of major corporations or banks used the most up-to-date architectural and engineering technologies to create striking results. These landmark buildings were designed to demonstrate the city's advance toward full development.

Index